LIFE ABOVE
the Negativity
from 10 minutes a day

Bible Versions Used

Our lives move at such a fast pace that we don't fully see the poor habits that have become a part of us. Its only when we pause and reflect on living intentionally that we see ourselves clearly. The Fast from Negativity will provide you with the tools you need to set healthy positive patterns in your life. What you discover about yourself may surprise you!

As you commit to living intentionally over the next 40 days, you will learn essential truths that will forever change your life. The key to the success of the Fast from Negativity is dependent upon your commitment to apply its truths. Anticipate the next 40 days to be an incredible life-transforming journey.

Kevin Fricker
Lead Pastor
City Centre Church
Edmonton AB Canada

It is good to see us being challenged to sincerely look at how we think, speak and live as Christians. In this book Trevor Lund touches on the "nitty-gritty" issues of how to develop our character to be more in line with what the Word of God says. Negative habits are not as easy to break as we might think. I know, because I had to make changes in the way I thought about myself, to bring my confession more into line with what God says about me. If we don't agree with the Word of God then we become the products of our own negative believing. And there are enough other people who can speak negative things about us without our having to add to it!

Three statements that especially stood out to me in this book are:

1. God's ways are not our ways. His thoughts are not our thoughts. His thoughts towards us are always good, because He is good. Good is not something God does, good is who He is.

2. Many times a critical person is someone with the gift of discernment who doesn't choose to operate in love.

3. Focus on what God has done and what He is doing. Take what He hasn't done to Him in prayer. He's there to comfort, but I've learned He really doesn't seem to respond well to whining.

May you be blessed and challenged as you take in, and respond to, the challenge of this book. It will change your life in a positive way.

Sincerely in Christ,

Rodney W. Francis

Founder/Director: The Gospel Faith Messenger Ministry (New Zealand)

Web Page: www.gospel.org.nz

When Adam and Eve sinned, in the Garden, the devil injected mankind with a deadly virus of negativity. A new language was born: unbelief, doubt, fear, and all kinds of negative thinking. It bogged the Israelites down for 40 years in the desert, and ever since, has had catastrophic influence upon the church. The one thing above all others that caused Jesus to be angry with his disciples was, doubt.

You would have thought that the followers of Him who declared, "All things are possible for those who believe" would all be possibility thinkers. But where are these? In science laboratories, space exploration projects, medical breakthrough experiments. All dedicated to doing that which hitherto has not been possible.

The church needs to wake up! Trevor has done a magnificent job challenging every believer to be a positive believer. I heartily recommend the book.

Wynne Lewis

From people who have fasted from negativity:

"While I was fasting from negativity, my supervisor gave me a gift certificate for $100 for being the most positive person in the company." (your results may vary)

"After the negativity fast my boss asked what my secret was for looking younger as I got older. I had to mention giving up negativity." (your results may vary)

LIFE ABOVE
the Negativity
from 10 minutes a day

By Trevor H Lund

IMAGINE
PUBLISHING.COM

ISBN -13 978-1-897409-16-9

Published through ImaginePublishing.com,

IMAGINE
PUBLISHING.COM

3428 – 99 Street Suite 444, Edmonton, Alberta, Canada, T6E 5X5
www.ImaginePublishing.com by Expectancy Ministries

ImaginePublishing.com cares about our environment. We plant three times the trees used to make this book. This is done to steward the resources the Father has provided.

First Printed as "40 Days From Negativity - an appetizer for life" 2007.

Second Edition 2008

Dedication

This book is dedicated to the love of my life and joy of my heart. God has shared His love of you with me, Kaz. May I always reflect His love to you. Thank you for your support, love and wisdom. The ministries that arise from this book are dedicated to the Father.

Expectancy Ministries

Expectancy Ministries is an Internet
and itinerant ministry that exists to
inspire individuals and empower their
dreams as they journey to and with
the Father, imparting to all revelation
of the goodness and greatness of God.

www.40DaysFromNegativity.com
 - daily encouragement to get rid of negativity

www.EncouragingEmails.com
 - receive emails when a blog from a ministry you
   support gets updated and automate your mailings
   from your ministry

www.DrinkFromTheDeep.com
 - experiencing more of our supernatural Father

www.EmpoweringInspiration.com
 - our 155,000+ item online bookstore

www.RevTrev.com
 -our prayer centre with info of the Lund's

http://streams.revtrev.com
 - our blog updated on the fly

http://LivingCreatively.RevTrev.com
 - our podcast

www.MiracleNewsToday.com
 - tell others or read about the wonders of our Good
   God

www.LifeAbovetheNegativity.com
 - resources for negativity fast campaigns

EXPECTANCY MINISTRIES
WE DELIVER
EXPECTANCYMINISTRIES.COM

Contents

Introduction

The negativity fast concept is not original with me. I know churches like Bethel in Redding, California have led people through it. My interest in fasting from negativity came as a response to a prophetic vision a friend in our church experienced.

She saw a giant wave of criticism about to crash on our city and church. It would seek to divide churches, leaders, congregations, friendships and marriages. Now this happens all around us, but I agreed with her sense that what was coming was to be bigger than simply more of the same. I told her to tell our pastor, after all, it's one of his jobs to protect the congregation.

But in the service that followed, the presence of God was palpable and as I was interceding for Pastor Kevin, the words "Negativity Fast" came to my mind. I didn't know much about it and so I decided to do some research.

To my shock, an online search for "negativity fast" brought up business gurus and New Age practitioners selling dubious products, but no references for Christians fasting from negativity. How could this be? We're the only ones with reasons not to be negative beyond "when you're positive, those around you will be positive" and "studies show positive people make more money and live longer." Hope is the helmet of our salvation. That means there can be no such thing as a pessimistic follower of Christ. We need to be positive because Christ is not negative.

But there are lies we believe that tell us we are the exception. There are circumstances that make it difficult. There are situations that make it seem impossible to abstain from being negative. The good news is that in Christ you can do all things.

As I studied what the Bible said, and prayed about what to do, God led me to approach my pastor with the idea for a "negativity fast." I would send out daily encouraging emails for 40 days. Every week, I'd produce and syndicate a podcast. Whenever I could, I'd write articles on various aspects of living above negativity.

Pastor Kevin showed great trust to allow me to do this. Thanks my friend, you have birthed more dreams in me. We had a few other churches join us immediately. A number more asked for the material for future campaigns.

This book is one of the two I wrote during those first 40 Days. I planned to only write one book, but isn't it amazing when you obey God's voice; He does things like doubling your effort.

This book allows you to go through your own 40 day negativity fast. It's always better if you can do this as a group, but there is great benefit even doing it solo. There's not much that you may not already know – except perhaps how to put it into practice. This is a tool for you to do just that.

Trevor H. Lund

September, 2007
ExpectancyMinistries.com

40DaysFromNegativity.com

This book was originally published at "40 Days From Negativity - an appetizer for life" We've included appendices in this edition to help you along your journey.

October 2008

Getting Acquainted with Key Concepts

from 10 minutes a day

So you've decided to take up a challenge that's too big not to die for, now what?

That's not meant to turn you back from the starting line, but it is to get you to count the costs before you begin. If you're feeling a little trepidation, that's OK. Read through this chapter and the next, but as you do, keep a couple of key thoughts in your mind.

First, God is more concerned about your character than your comfort. His goal is to conform you into the likeness of His son (Romans 8:29). Yes, He loves you the way you are, but He loves you too much to let you stay that way. You have too many people to impact for His Kingdom that you can't influence until more of Christ is seen in you.

I'm not writing to brand-new followers of Christ here. It's not just the newly-planted that need deeper roots. Even if you're a tree planted by the river of God whose leaves produce fruit in their season, your roots need to continue to reach towards the rich nutrients the river brings. Your branches need to continue to stretch towards the life-giving sun.

> God is more concerned about your character than your comfort

A tree grows towards the light, but it will never reach the sun. We're all on a journey and we'll never be able to say, "I've arrived." Nebuchadnezzar said that while on a roof in Babylon, and look what happened the next seven years of his life.

So remember, all of us can become more like Christ – that's the great adventure we're on.

Secondly, as you read these introductory chapters, realize you can do all things through Christ who strengthens you. The work that He's begun in you, He'll be faithful to complete. God doesn't give you a test so you can fail. Even though negativity is one of the toughest things you can fast from, you can do it! The same power that raised Jesus from the dead is alive within you (Ephesians 1:17-20).

With these thoughts in mind, let's examine some of the questions around a fast from negativity.

What is a Negativity Fast?

A "fast" is abstaining from something – usually food – for spiritual reasons, for a given reason and set period of time.

Daniel fasted from wine, meat and choice foods for 21 days when he was awaiting an answer from God. Jesus fasted from food for 40 days at the start of His ministry.

Isaiah 58 lays out the kind of fast that is acceptable to God and the blessing that comes from that kind of fast.

> 'We have fasted before you!' they say.
>   'Why aren't you impressed?
> We have been very hard on ourselves,
>   and you don't even notice it!'
> "I will tell you why!" I respond.
>   "It's because you are fasting to please yourselves.
>   Even while you fast,
>   you keep oppressing your workers.
>   What good is fasting

when you keep on fighting and
quarreling?
  This kind of fasting
    will never get you anywhere with me.
  You humble yourselves
    by going through the motions of
penance,
    bowing your heads
      like reeds bending in the wind.
  You dress in burlap
    and cover yourselves with ashes.
  Is this what you call fasting?
    Do you really think this will please
the Lord?
  "No, this is the kind of fasting I want:
    Free those who are wrongly
imprisoned;
      lighten the burden of those who work
for you.
  Let the oppressed go free,
    and remove the chains that bind
people.
  Share your food with the hungry,
    and give shelter to the homeless.
  Give clothes to those who need them,
    and do not hide from relatives who
need your help.
  "Then your salvation will come like the
dawn,
    and your wounds will quickly heal.
  Your godliness will lead you forward,
    and the glory of the Lord will protect
you from behind. Then when you call, the
Lord will answer.
    'Yes, I am here,' he will quickly reply.
  "Remove the heavy yoke of oppression.
    Stop pointing your finger and

spreading vicious rumors!
 Feed the hungry, and help those in
trouble.
 Then your light will shine out from the
darkness,
 and the darkness around you will be
as bright as noon.
 The Lord will guide you continually,
 giving you water when you are dry
 and restoring your strength.
 You will be like a well-watered garden,
 like an ever-flowing spring.
 Some of you will rebuild the deserted
ruins of your cities.
 Then you will be known as a rebuilder
of walls
 and a restorer of homes.
 "Keep the Sabbath day holy.
 Don't pursue your own interests on
that day,
 but enjoy the Sabbath
 and speak of it with delight as the
Lord's holy day.
 Honor the Sabbath in everything you
do on that day, and don't follow your
own desires or talk idly.
 Then the Lord will be your delight.
 I will give you great honor
 and satisfy you with the inheritance I
promised to your ancestor Jacob.
 I, the Lord, have spoken!" (NLT)

This is how we fast when we fast from negativity.

We've defined "negativity" as "any thought, word, or action that is contrary to the will of God expressed in Scripture."

Bill Johnson, pastor of Bethel Church in Redding,

California says: "I cannot afford to have any thought in my head that's not His." This applies to all of us. Thoughts lead to words and actions so the main battlefield when we fast from negativity will be our minds.

> We've defined "negativity" as "any thought, word, or action that is contrary to the will of God expressed in Scripture."

We fast from negativity because we want our thoughts, words and actions to reflect the goodness and greatness of God.

Why should I fast for 40 days from negativity?

Some individuals correctly point out that our thoughts, words and actions should always reflect God's goodness and greatness. We are followers of Christ, after all.

I prefer to think of the 40-Days approach as an offer of amnesty. The police in Canada will often hold a "turn-in-your-illegal-weapons-without-being-charged" campaign to get unregistered weapons away from the potential of theft. A 40 day fast gives followers of Christ the opportunity to act more like Christ without the condemnation that they haven't been consistently acting like Christ.

Secondly, it takes 21 days to form a habit, but our goal is to shape our character. Having positive thoughts, words and actions for 40 days gives us great opportunity to shape our character. Fasting from negativity for 40 days should get you to the place where not being negative becomes a natural part of your life. Tricking yourself into starting is a great way to get any goal accomplished.

from 10 minutes a day

When should I fast from negativity?

Don't wait until you feel like abstaining from any thought, word or action that is contrary to the will of God expressed in Scripture. It's a decision you need to make ahead of time.

Don't set your alarm for 5 AM and leave the decision if you'll get up when the alarm goes off to when the alarm goes off. Your intention of spending time alone with God will never amount to action until you make the decision ahead of time to make the time.

There will be ample times when conditions will be conducive for you to choose to be negative over the next 40 days. Your decision to fast from negativity, the power of the Holy Spirit, and knowledge that with every temptation God provides a way out of that temptation, will be what stops you from choosing to be negative when conditions are conducive.

> Can you tell God when and how you'll be obedient to Him?

If you're putting off bringing every thought captive and making obedient to Christ, you need to consider something very carefully. Can you tell God when and how you'll be obedient to Him?

Saul tried to keep the best of the Amalekite animals, saying they would be a sacrifice to God. But he disobeyed God's command to completely destroy this people whose sin reached its full measure. Samuel's response was:

> "What is more pleasing to the Lord:
> your burnt offerings and sacrifices
> or your obedience to his voice?

Listen! Obedience is better than sacrifice,
and submission is better than offering the fat of rams.
Rebellion is as sinful as witchcraft,
and stubbornness as bad as worshiping idols.
So because you have rejected the command of the Lord,
he has rejected you as king."
1 Samuel 15:22-23 (New Living Translation)

Don't make excuses to allow negativity to remain in your life.

LIFE ABOVE the Negativity

Examining
Scripture

As you consider fasting from negativity, it's good we share some of the scriptures you can investigate. Study the context of these verses. Ask more mature followers of Christ to help you understand what they mean. These verses come without commentary, so ask the Holy Spirit to teach you all things as you let the Word read you. We've used a variety of translations to get you to think about verses in different ways.

Don't excuse yourself from putting them into practice, but pray about how you can work them into your life. Know that this list is not all encompassing. God may be asking more of you than what I've come up with in my study.

So let's look at the thoughts, words and actions the Bible says we should abstain from.

Thoughts to abstain from:

And then he added, "It is what comes from inside that defiles you. For from within, out of a person's heart, come evil thoughts, sexual immorality, theft, murder, adultery, greed, wickedness, deceit, lustful desires, envy, slander, pride, and foolishness. All these vile things come from within; they are what defile you."
Mark 7:20-23 (NLT)

Self-Condemnation

Above all else, guard your heart,
for it is the wellspring of life.
Proverbs 4:23 (NIV)

Un-forgiveness

Bear with each other and forgive
whatever grievances you may have
against one another. Forgive as the Lord
forgave you.
Colossians 3:13 (NIV)

Being Offended at God

And blessed is he who is not offended
because of Me.
Luke 7:23 (NKJV)

Judgmental Attitudes

Who are you to judge someone else's
servant? To his own master he stands or
falls. And he will stand, for the Lord is
able to make him stand.
Romans 14:4 (NIV)

Rebellion

Make the Master proud of you by being
good citizens. Respect the authorities,
whatever their level; they are God's
emissaries for keeping order. It is God's
will that by doing good, you might cure
the ignorance of the fools who think
you're a danger to society. Exercise your
freedom by serving God, not by breaking
the rules. Treat everyone you meet with
dignity. Love your spiritual family. Revere

LIFE ABOVE the Negativity

God. Respect the government. 1 Peter 2:13-17 (The Message)

Fear

For God has not given us a spirit of fearfulness, but one of power, love, and sound judgment. 2 Timothy 1:7 (HCSB)

Worry

For this reason I say to you, do not be worried about your life, as to what you will eat or what you will drink; nor for your body, as to what you will put on. Is not life more than food, and the body more than clothing?
Look at the birds of the air, that they do not sow, nor reap nor gather into barns, and yet your heavenly Father feeds them. Are you not worth much more than they?
"And who of you by being worried can add a single hour to his life?
"And why are you worried about clothing? Observe how the lilies of the field grow; they do not toil nor do they spin, yet I say to you that not even Solomon in all his glory clothed himself like one of these."
Matthew 6:25-29 (NASB)

Pride

Do not be wise in your own eyes. Fear the Lord and turn away from what is sinful. Proverbs 3:7 (New Life Version)

from 10 minutes a day

Bitterness

> *Get rid of all bitterness, rage and anger, brawling and slander, along with every form of malice. Ephesians 4:31 (NIV)*

Discouragement

> *Do not let this Book of the Law depart from your mouth; meditate on it day and night, so that you may be careful to do everything written in it. Then you will be prosperous and successful. Have I not commanded you? Be strong and courageous. Do not be terrified; do not be discouraged, for the LORD your God will be with you wherever you go. Joshua 1:8-9 (New International Version)*

Feeling Overwhelmed

> *But now, O Jacob, listen to the Lord who created you.*
> *O Israel, the one who formed you says,*
> *"Do not be afraid, for I have ransomed you. I have called you by name; you are mine.*
> *When you go through deep waters,*
> *I will be with you.*
> *When you go through rivers of difficulty,*
> *you will not drown.*
> *When you walk through the fire of oppression,*
> *you will not be burned up;*
> *the flames will not consume you.*
> *Isaiah 43:1-2 (NLT)*

LIFE ABOVE the Negativity

Condemnation

Therefore, there is now no condemnation for those who are in Christ Jesus, Romans 8:1 (NIV)

Anxiousness

Do not be anxious about anything, but in everything, by prayer and petition, with thanksgiving, present your requests to God.
Philippians 4:6 (NIV)

Anxiety

Cast all your anxiety on him because he cares for you.
1 Peter 5:7 (NIV)

Words to Abstain From:

The tongue also is a fire, a world of evil among the parts of the body. It corrupts the whole person, sets the whole course of his life on fire, and is itself set on fire by hell. James 3:6 (NIV)

Careless Words

A good man produces good things from his storeroom of good, and an evil man produces evil things from his storeroom of evil. I tell you that on the day of judgment people will have to account for every careless word they speak. For by your words you will be acquitted, and by your words you will be condemned. Matthew 12:35-37 (HCSB)

"Loose" Words

*When words are many, sin is not absent,
but he who holds his tongue is wise.
Proverbs 10:19 (NIV)*

Angry words spoken in haste

*Understand this, my dear brothers and
sisters: You must all be quick to listen,
slow to speak, and slow to get angry.
James 1:19 (NLT)*

Cutting Words

*Some people make cutting remarks,
but the words of the wise bring
healing.
Proverbs 12:18 (NLT)*

Discouraging Words

*Why do you discourage the Israelites from
going over into the land the LORD has
given them? Numbers 32:7 (NIV)*

Lies

*Therefore each of you must put off
falsehood and speak truthfully to his
neighbor, for we are all members of one
body.
Ephesians 4:25 (NIV)*

Complaining and Arguing

*Do everything without complaining and
arguing, so that no one can criticize you.*

LIFE ABOVE the Negativity

*Live clean, innocent lives as children of
God, shining like bright lights in a world
full of crooked and perverse people. Hold
firmly to the word of life; then, on the day
of Christ's return, I will be proud that I did
not run the race in vain and that my work
was not useless.*
Philippians 2:14-16 (NLT)

Slander

*Get rid of all bitterness, rage and anger,
brawling and slander, along with every
form of malice.*
Ephesians 4:31 (NIV)

Obscenity, Foolish Talk, Course Joking

*Nor should there be obscenity, foolish
talk or coarse joking, which are out of
place, but rather thanksgiving.*
Ephesians 5:4 (NIV)

Foul or Abusive Words

*Don't use foul or abusive language.
Let everything you say be good and
helpful, so that your words will be an
encouragement to those who hear them.*
Ephesians 4:29 (NLT)

Words of Dissension

*A perverse man stirs up dissension,
and a gossip separates close friends.*
Proverbs 16:28 (NIV)

Gossip

> *A gossip goes around telling secrets,*
> so don't hang around with chatterers.
>> *Proverbs 20:19 (NLT)*

Actions to Abstain From:

> *For you are free, yet you are God's slaves,*
> *so don't use your freedom as an excuse*
> *to do evil.*
> *1 Peter 2:16 (NLT)*

Quarrelling, Factions, Arrogance

> *For I am afraid that when I come I may*
> *not find you as I want you to be, and*
> *you may not find me as you want me to*
> *be. I fear that there may be quarreling,*
> *jealousy, outbursts of anger, factions,*
> *slander, gossip, arrogance and disorder.*
> *2 Corinthians 12:20 (NIV)*

Sexual Immorality

> *Let there be no sexual immorality,*
> *impurity, or greed among you. Such sins*
> *have no place among God's people.*
> *Ephesians 5:3 (NLT)*

Busy-ness

> *"Come to me, all you who are weary and*
> *burdened, and I will give you rest. Take*
> *my yoke upon you and learn from me, for*
> *I am gentle and humble in heart, and you*
> *will find rest for your souls. For my yoke is*
> *easy and my burden is light."*
> *Matthew 11:28-30 (NIV)*

from 10 minutes a day

Instead of focusing on what we shouldn't be thinking or saying or doing, let's spend some time examining Scripture to see what we should be filling our conversation with.

What we should think about is summed up in Philippians 4:8; how we can change our thinking is found in Romans 12:1-2. How we should live is found throughout Scripture so we'll limit this discussion to words that bring life. This is not a definitive list; it is truth that speaks to me.

Words that Bring Life

Simon Peter answered him, "Lord, to whom shall we go? You have the words of eternal life."
John 6:68 (NIV)

Healing Words

Reckless words pierce like a sword, but the tongue of the wise brings healing.
Proverbs 12:18 (NIV)

Kind Words

An anxious heart weighs a man down, but a kind word cheers him up.
Proverbs 12:25 (NIV)

Gentle Words

A gentle answer turns away wrath, but a harsh word stirs up anger.
Proverbs 15:1 (NIV)

Pleasant Words

> *Pleasant words are a honeycomb,*
> *sweet to the soul and healing to the*
> *bones.*
> *Proverbs 16:24 (NIV)*

Patient Words

> *Through patience a ruler can be*
> *persuaded,*
> *and a gentle tongue can break a*
> *bone. Proverbs 25:15 (NIV)*

Thankful Words

> *Obscene stories, foolish talk, and coarse*
> *jokes—these are not for you. Instead, let*
> *there be thankfulness to God.*
> *Ephesians 5:4 (NLT)*

Encouraging Words

> *Do not let any unwholesome talk come*
> *out of your mouths, but only what is*
> *helpful for building others up according*
> *to their needs, that it may benefit those*
> *who listen. Ephesians 4:29 (NIV)*

Words of Truth

> *What this adds up to, then, is this: no*
> *more lies, no more pretense. Tell your*
> *neighbor the truth. In Christ's body we're*
> *all connected to each other, after all.*
> *When you lie to others, you end up lying*
> *to yourself.*
> *Ephesians 4:25 (The Message)*

from 10 minutes a day

31

LIFE ABOVE the Negativity

Words in Love

*Instead, speaking the truth in love, we
will in all things grow up into him who is
the Head, that is, Christ.*
Ephesians 4:15 (NIV)

Words of Praise

Sing to the LORD, you saints of his;
praise his holy name.
Psalm 30:4 (NIV)

Words Without Deceit

Yes, what joy for those
whose record the Lord has cleared
of guilt,whose lives are lived in complete
honesty!
Psalm 32:2 (NLT)

Words that Sustain the Weary

The Sovereign Lord has given me
his words of wisdom, so that I know how
to comfort the weary.
Morning by morning he wakens me
and opens my understanding to his
will.
Isaiah 50:4 (NLT)

Words of Invitation

*I pray that you may be active in sharing
your faith, so that you will have a full
understanding of every good thing we
have in Christ.*
Philemon 1:6 (NIV)

Strategies for the Battlegrounds You're About to Face

Those who live only to satisfy their own sinful nature will harvest decay and death from that sinful nature. But those who live to please the Spirit will harvest everlasting life from the Spirit. Galatians 6:8 (NLT)

It's good to know the lay of the land before you begin any battle. And this is a battle you're about to enter. We've outlined where most of the battles are fought and provided proven strategies to win those battles with the help of the Holy Spirit.

A Negativity Fast has two areas of confrontation that you need to be ready for, before you go into it. The first controls the second, but one cannot be dealt with, without dealing with the other. These areas are your mind, (a.k.a. heart), and your mouth.

Our Mind

In our mind there are at least six strongholds that are common to many: self-condemnation, living in a negative environment, excusing un-forgiveness, living offended at God, wallowing in discouragement, and being judgmental.

LIFE ABOVE the Negativity

Self-Condemnation

We all have lies we believe. These lies come in to help us "heal" wounds that we've been afflicted with. It's not actual healing that occurs; it's a snare of the enemy to gain a stronghold in our lives.

Try this exercise:

1. List 10 words of affirmation that have stuck with you ever since you first heard them.

2. Now list 10 words of death that have stuck with you ever since you first heard them.

3. Which list was easier to recall?

4. Which list had more emotional triggers?

Living in a fallen world, and living with fallen people, we've all been wounded. Lies are what others have told us as we've grown up. They may not have been spoken to us directly, but we've internalized them nonetheless. They are deceitful, downgrading and condemning.

"I can't do it."

"I'm worthless."

"I'm stupid."

"I'm ugly."

"I'm useless."

They are so much a part of us that until we can see the lies, we won't know we have them. We won't know to see them, until we know who we are in Christ.

> Living in a fallen world, and living with fallen people, we've all been wounded.

In Christ, there is no more condemnation (Romans 8:1) so we know the thoughts that we are condemned with are not his.

The power of God can set you free of the chains of condemnation. This is your part to play:

> *For though we live in the world, we*
> *do not wage war as the world does.*
> *The weapons we fight with are not the*
> *weapons of the world. On the contrary,*
> *they have divine power to demolish*
> *strongholds. We demolish arguments and*
> *every pretension that sets itself up against*
> *the knowledge of God, and we take*
> *captive every thought to make it obedient*
> *to Christ. 2 Corinthians 10:3-5 (NIV)*

You heal the wounds the lies have joined with by choosing to believe and live out of the truth.

How do you do that?

If you haven't done it before – ask God to forgive you for living out of the lies instead of the truth of how He sees you. When you confess your sins, He forgives you (1 John 1:9). So when the thoughts come back – and they will - this is a process – reject them. Do it out loud if you can: "I don't accept that. It's not who God says I am."

Next, replace the lie with the truth from God's word. Let's take a few examples, and use the tool provide by Neil T. Anderson:

| "I can't do it." | I can do all things through Christ who strengthens me. (Philippians 4:13) |
| | The same power that raised Christ Jesus from the dead is alive in me. (Eph. 1:19-20) |

LIFE ABOVE the Negativity

"I'm worthless."	I have been justified (Romans 5:1)
	I am united with the Lord and I am one spirit with Him (1Cor 6:17)
	I have been bought with a price; I belong to God (1Cor 6:19,20)
"I'm stupid."	I am the salt of the earth and the light of the world (Mat 5:13,14)
	I am a branch of the true vine, a channel of His life (John 15:1,5)
	I have been chosen and appointed by God to bear fruit (John 15:6)
	I am a personal, Spirit-empowered witness of Christ's (Acts 1:8)
	I am a temple of God (1 Corinthians 3:16)
"I'm ugly."	I am free forever from condemnation (Romans 8:1,2)
	I am free from any condemning charges against me (Rom 8:31-34)

"I'm useless."	I am a temple of God (1 Corinthians 3:16)
	I am a minister of reconciliation for God (2 Corinthians 5:17-21)
	I am God's co-worker (2 Corinthians 6:1)
	I am seated with Christ in the heavenly realms (Ephesians 2:6)
	I am God's workmanship, created for good works (Ephesians 2:10)

You'll find over time the Spirit will make these truths self-evident. If your wounds are deep, seek out more mature believers to help walk you through the pain of the past. Someone with Theophostic or Sozo training will help facilitate the Spirit's healing in your life.

There's another key that John gives to overcoming self-criticism. You're going to discover love is the antidote to every type of negativity. This is also true with negative self-talk that arises out of worry. See how Peterson transliterates 1 John 3:18-20:

> My dear children, let's not just talk about love; let's practice real love. This is the only way we'll know we're living truly, living in God's reality. It's also the way to shut down debilitating self-criticism, even when there is something to it. For God is greater than our worried hearts and knows more about us than we do ourselves. (The Message)

LIFE ABOVE the Negativity

Stop the negative self-talk when you fast from negativity.

Living in a Negative Environment

If you can do a Negativity Fast with your family and co-workers and church, you are so much further ahead than if you are surrounded with others who are negative.

Can you limit yourself to negative exposure? Sometimes you'll need to walk away. We all have to at times. We live in a society that lives with the credo: "if it bleeds, it leads." When something affects you negatively, even if it's on the news, take it to God in prayer and/or turn it off. If you get angry reading the newspaper, put the paper away. I'm not espousing, "ignorance is bliss". If we'd pray about the news that bothers us, we'd change the news.

Do other drivers set you off? If everyone who drives too slowly is a menace and everyone who passes you is a maniac, you'll need to adjust your attitude. Give yourself more time to get places and make it a practice to bless those who curse you.

> ...it's not as if you can cut yourself off from your life. Nor should you.

However, if the negative environment you're in is your spouse or family or workplace or church family – it's not as if you can cut yourself off from your life. Nor should you.

You are the salt of the world and light of the earth. You preserve and illuminate that of which you are a part. The gates of hell cannot prevail against you, but your path will be a little more troubled.

You need to live the promise of Isaiah 26:3:

> *You will keep in perfect peace all who*
> *trust in you, all whose thoughts are fixed*
> *on you! (NLT)*

How can you do this? Learn how to practice the presence of God.

Brother Lawrence was a 16th century Carmelite monk. Having never studied for the ministry he was only accepted as a lay brother and kept in lowly positions. Yet despite, or perhaps because of that, many were attracted to his character. He was known for his profound peace.

He wrote in what would become "The Practice of the Presence of God":

> "As often as I could, I placed myself as a worshiper before him, fixing my mind upon his holy presence, recalling it when I found it wandering from him. This proved to be an exercise frequently painful, yet I persisted through all difficulties."

Yet he persisted and later could say:

> "I began to live as if there were no one save God and me in the world."

Regardless of your environment, you can fast from negativity. Paul gives this advice to the church in Philippi:

And now, dear brothers and sisters, one final thing. Fix your thoughts on what is true, and honorable, and right, and pure, and lovely, and admirable. Think about things that are excellent and worthy of praise. Keep putting into practice all you learned and received from me— everything you heard from me and saw me doing. Then the God of peace will be with you. Philippians 4:8-9 (NLT)

As you fill yourself with the true and honorable and right and pure and lovely and admirable, recognize God is always everywhere and then choose to live as if God is always everywhere.

This may only be encouraging when you grasp that God is good and desires good for His children.

When you live within a negative environment, you need to live with the understanding given to us by JB Philips' translation of Romans 12:1-3:

"Don't let the world around you squeeze you into its own mold, but let God remold your minds from within, so that you may prove in practice that the plan of God for you is good, meets all his demands, and moves toward the goal of true maturity" (Romans 12:1-3; Phillips)

Don't use your negative environment as an excuse to remain negative. As a child of the one who created the weather, you bring your own weather wherever you go. As you allow God to renew your mind from within, you will begin to change the world around you. How's that for a negativity fast challenge?

from 10 minutes a day

Excusing Un-forgiveness

Hurt people hurt people and no doubt, hurt people have hurt you. Forgiveness is a choice we need to make. The only one you hurt is yourself when you choose not to forgive. Forgiveness leaves the issue with God. He's the one who will avenge. He's the one who will repay. Forgiveness does not let the other off the hook; it puts them into God's capable hands. You must choose to forgive as Christ forgave us – while we were still sinners, he died for us (Romans 5:8).

Before you begin the Negativity Fast, ask God to reveal anyone you need to forgive, then choose to forgive them. Will the feelings go away? Not at first. But here's some advice from a booklet I've written *"The Freedom of Forgiveness"* that's available at www.EmpoweringInspiration.com:

If I can't forget, does that mean I haven't forgiven?

No. God does not forget the sins He forgives us of…

He chooses instead to not remember and hold them against us.

"For I will forgive their wickedness and will remember their sins no more."(Jeremiah 31:34 NIV)

Then he adds: "Their sins and lawless acts I will remember no more."(Hebrews 10:17 NIV)

Is this important?

Yes.

We also can't easily forget. God has created us with minds to remember. Thoughts will pop back into our minds and we have no power over the past - but we do have control over how we let our past control our present and our future.

> Hurt people hurt people and no doubt, hurt people have hurt you.

So is there any hope?

YES!

When memories come, of hurts and pains you have chosen to forgive, don't try to ignore them. Remember the whole event - including the FACT you have forgiven them with the strength God provides.

Dr. Chuck Lynch in his book *"I Should Forgive But…"* gives this advice regarding the obsessive thinking that often surrounds even forgiven hurts:

1. ***Address God*** - Stating God's name in a firm way forcibly stops the obsessive thinking, but usually only momentarily. It is the starting point for dealing with dangerous thoughts.

2.***Thank God*** - Express appreciation to God for allowing you to remember the past offense you had to forgive. This allows you to review this biblical tool which Christ illustrated at the time of His own hurt and rejection "Father, forgive them…" It will also bring to mind that you have left them with God. You can thank Him that you were able to give the same gift of forgiveness you received and thus reflect God's character to others.

3.***Praise God*** - Sincerely praise God for the tool of forgiveness. Praise Him for forgiving you as you forgive others and for what He's going to do through this experience for His glory.

This is a proven strategy for experiencing the freedom of forgiveness. As you fast from negativity, you need to forgive the wrongs done to you. Over the next forty days we'll explain more.

LIFE ABOVE the Negativity

Living Offended at God

In the battle for your mind, you also need to choose to live un-offended at God.

John the Baptist declared the Lamb of God who takes away the sin of the world and then sat in prison awaiting his fate. He sent his disciples to ask his cousin if he had gotten it right and Jesus responded:

> *"Go and tell John the things you have*
> *seen and heard: that the blind see, the*
> *lame walk, the lepers are cleansed,*
> *the deaf hear, the dead are raised, the*
> *poor have the gospel preached to them.*
> *And blessed is he who is not offended*
> *because of Me." Luke 7:22-23 (NKJV)*

John was sitting where he did not expect, facing something he did not want. We could almost say he had the right to be offended at Jesus.

In our journey with God we'll have similar experiences. The choice will be ours to live un-offended towards God. We need to choose to give up our "right" to understand. If you haven't made these choices, the Negativity Fast is an excellent opportunity to ask God to forgive you and to ask the Holy Spirit to empower you to embrace the peace that passes understanding.

God's ways are not our ways. His thoughts are not our thoughts. His thoughts towards us are always good, because He is good. Good is not something God does, good is who He is.

Trust Him with your life and live a blessed life by not being

> The choice will be ours to live un-offended towards God.

44

offended because of Him. Don't worry, we take more time to explain this better during the 40 days.

Wallowing in Discouragement

We can choose to wallow in discouragement by simply not realizing it is a battle for our mind. We live in a fallen world where God's will is not done as it is in Heaven and we live with fallen people who do all sorts of evil.

Our choice is between life and death (see Proverbs 18:21).

David faced a similar choice. His company returned to Ziklag to find it pillaged and their wives and children carried off. He was distressed and the men talked about stoning him.

> *But David strengthened himself in the LORD his God. 1 Samuel 30:6 (NKJV)*

When you feel discouraged – and you will – choose to strengthen yourself in the Lord. Why not pray as David prayed? Why not pray the Psalms? God has given us a language to pour our hearts out to Him. Take Psalm 13 as an example:

> *How long, O LORD ? Will you forget me forever?*
> *How long will you hide your face from me?*
> *How long must I wrestle with my thoughts*
> *and every day have sorrow in my heart?*
> *How long will my enemy triumph over me?*

from 10 minutes a day

Look on me and answer, O LORD my God.
Give light to my eyes, or I will sleep in death;
my enemy will say, "I have overcome him,"
and my foes will rejoice when I fall.
But I trust in your unfailing love;
my heart rejoices in your salvation.
I will sing to the LORD,
for he has been good to me. (NIV)

Notice a couple of things. First, David doesn't hold back his feelings. He lays it all out on the line. We don't need to put on a mask to have a Negativity Fast. God isn't interested in our being actors. We don't ignore our feelings or the situation. We don't stick our head in the sand and hope it all goes away.

But notice something else in this Psalm. David doesn't end it after the fourth verse. Two-thirds of the Psalms are psalms of lament and almost all of them don't stop with the lament.

> ...choose to strengthen yourself in the Lord.

Too often we do. We wallow in the discouragement.

But to strengthen ourselves in the Lord, we need to turn our focus back to God. We need to remember what He has done for us. We need to testify about His goodness. We need to tell God the truth about Himself – that's a great definition for praise.

Your conversation is between God and you. Keep your lament in perspective. Your words can discourage another. Be completely honest before

God and wise in your words towards other and your life may just change during the next 40 days.

Being Judgmental

Are you quick to pass judgment on another? Who are you to judge someone else's servant? (Romans 14:4) Many times a critical person is someone with the gift of discernment who doesn't choose to operate in love.

Jesus said to "Judge not" and was speaking about a critical spirit (Luke 6:37). Paul said that we'll judge angels and was making an argument for maturing in the faith (1 Corinthians 6:2-4). The two don't contradict each other, because both imply we shouldn't operate outside of love. Love is the antidote for being judgmental.

So how do you love?

It starts with a decision to grow in the fruit of the Spirit (Galatians 5:22-23). Since the fruit of the Spirit reflects the nature of Christ in us, we know it pleases God for us to continue to grow in it.

Verbalize that choice every morning. "I am not my own, I am bought with a price, I belong to God. I choose to grow in and put on love, joy, peace, patience, kindness, goodness, faithfulness, gentleness and self-control."

Then recognize when God is giving you opportunity to choose to grow in these areas. This is how you do it:

> Love is the antidote for being judgmental.

Fruit naturally grows when the branch it's on is attached to the vine. Jesus is the vine, and we are the branches. As we abide in Him and spend time with Him, we naturally begin to reflect His glory more and more.

Jesus sums it all up in John 15:5-15:

"I am the vine; you are the branches. If a man remains in me and I in him, he will bear much fruit; apart from me you can do nothing. If anyone does not remain in me, he is like a branch that is thrown away and withers; such branches are picked up, thrown into the fire and burned. If you remain in me and my words remain in you, ask whatever you wish, and it will be given you. This is to my Father's glory, that you bear much fruit, showing yourselves to be my disciples.

"As the Father has loved me, so have I loved you. Now remain in my love. If you obey my commands, you will remain in my love, just as I have obeyed my Father's commands and remain in his love. I have told you this so that my joy may be in you and that your joy may be complete. My command is this: Love each other as I have loved you. Greater love has no one than this, that he lay down his life for his friends. You are my friends if you do what I command. I no longer call you servants, because a servant does not know his master's business. Instead, I have called you friends, for everything that I learned from my Father I have made known to you."

So as you choose love, you abide in Christ and

His words abide in you. You can't be judgmental of someone else's servant when you make the decision to love. Lose the judgmental attitude as you fast from negativity.

Our Mouths

The next area of confrontation you'll face in a Negativity Fast is what comes out of your mouth. This is the area that is most visible to people who are watching you and your witness of Christ. Proverbs 18:21 gives us hope that we can control our tongues:

> "The tongue has the power of life and death, and those who love it will eat its fruit." (NIV)

How do you choose to speak the words of life?

Choose Life

First of all, commit yourself to controlling your tongue. Declare it to God every morning:

> Though you probe my heart and examine me at night, though you test me, you will find nothing; I have resolved that my mouth will not sin. Psalm 17:3 (NIV)

In a little bit, we'll give you a tool to help you choose life in the moment-to-moment situations, but there is something to choosing to speak life at the start of the day.

Control Your Thoughts

The battle for our minds is such a vicious battle that we need to take up our positions, stand firm and see the deliverance of the Lord. In Proverbs declares:

> Above all else, guard your heart, for it is
> the wellspring of life. Proverbs 4:23 (NIV)

Your mind is the first and greatest battlefield as you fast from negativity. Jesus said in Matthew 12:34:

> For out of the overflow of the heart the
> mouth speaks. (NIV)

So it's not as if you can control your mouth without also controlling what's in your heart. We've already said a lot about this, so not much more needs to be said. Stop the negative, critical, judgmental thinking and it will stop seeping out of your mouth. If you don't control your thinking, you can't control your tongue.

> So it's not as if you can control your mouth without also controlling what's in your heart.

With the Holy Spirit, you can do it.

Change Your Behavior

But don't think you can wait to clean up the inside before you worry about the outside. You'll wound many people before you clean up your act. Take responsibility for your actions.

And here's a secret: your actions help shape your attitudes.

For too long, changing the actions of people is all the church has emphasized. As long as others did what we told them was right, we were satisfied all was right between them and God. But God cares too much about us to be satisfied with us going through the motions.

> ...your actions help shape your attitudes.

And though our tendency is to throw the baby out with bathwater, don't live as if you can wait to be obedient to God. Remember the Golden Rule:

> Do to others as you would have them do
> to you. Matthew 7:12(NIV)

And since you know this one, another one is applicable.

> "Anyone, then who knows the good
> he ought to do and doesn't do it, sins."
> James 4:17 (NIV)

Stop Unwholesome Flows

How do you put the Golden Rule into practice with regards to your mouth? Instead of listening to my suggestions, live what the Bible says:

> Do not let any unwholesome talk come out of your mouths, but only what is helpful for building others up according to their needs, that it may benefit those who listen. And do not grieve the Holy Spirit of God, with whom you where sealed for the day of redemption. Get rid of all bitterness, rage anger, brawling and slander, along with every form of malice. Be kind and compassionate to one another, forgiving one each other, just as in Christ God forgave you. Ephesians 4:29-32 (NIV)

Speak the Truth in Love

Avoiding conflict is not a virtue. You aren't showing love to a friend when you let them continue in sin. But some people feel that the truth needs to hurt.

> You're not in the right place if you enjoy putting someone in his or her place.

A basic rule of confrontation is "If it doesn't hurt you to say something difficult, don't say it." You're not in the right place if you enjoy putting someone in his or her place.

Truth must always be spoken in love:

> *Speaking the truth in love, we will in all*
> *things grow up into him who is the Head,*
> *that is, Christ.*   Ephesians 4:15 (NIV)

Be Accountable

By having a friend, or fiancée, co-worker or spouse ask you a few simple questions, or tell you when they see you doing any of these things, you'll stay on the transformational path.

Just for fun, tell your co-workers or spouse to let you know when they hear words like "Stupid" or "Loser" come out of your mouth. They'll have fun with it and you'll learn to be more careful. It can be an excellent witness to your pre-Christian co-workers. Tell them you're trying to become more like Jesus.

Record the times you mess up. You'll see the grace God has for you and find it easier to extend that grace to others.

However, too often accountability focuses on the negative – we go over a bunch of sins we've already confessed to God. During Negativity Fast, why not be held accountable to be positive?   Here's what I mean.

Use your time with an accountability partner to speak positively about the good things of God. Don't go over all the times you've failed. A simple, "I've had a good day" or "I need some encouragement today" will suffice. Keeping the record is for you alone. Talk to your accountability partner about whatever is true, whatever is noble, whatever is right, whatever is pure, whatever is lovely, whatever is admirable - anything that is excellent or praiseworthy, and you'll both be

from 10 minutes a day

encouraged to stay on the path.

Here are some questions you may choose to have them ask you:

1. What's been a struggle you've had with negativity this week?

2. What has God been teaching you about yourself?

3. How are you developing the gifts/dreams God has given you?

Accountability is a great tool to assure success in your fast from negativity.

Be Prepared

When others give you the opportunity to choose to be negative, or invite you to join in their cynicism, you need to choose to pause and think of something positive to say.

It's not always going to be easy. Can you imagine someone coming up to you with a complaint like this?

"Can you believe so-and-so didn't come see my neighbour when she was in the hospital? He/she knew I was too uncomfortable to go myself. Why, he/she didn't even return my phone call."

Now your mutual 'friend' also didn't return your phone call, so how do you respond?

Pause. – Don't let your first thought be the first thing out of your mouth. (Psalm 37:30)

Pray. – Ask God for wisdom (James 1:5). Ask Christ for the words of life. (John 6:68). Ask the Holy Spirit to teach you what to say (Luke 12:12).

Please. –Please GOD. Only let what comes out of your mouth be for edification or encouragement. (Ephesians 4:29)

You have that already mastered? Great. Let's move on to something that can be even more challenging – gossip.

Stop Gossiping

Since gossip is about other people's problems, it's inherently rife with negativity. During your fast, choose to stop it.

Stop the person sharing "news" or "prayer items". They are only inviting you to participate in the negativity feast. Simply tell them: "We're not part of the solution or part of the problem, so we don't discuss it or make judgments." Then tell them to confess their sin of gossip to God and pray with them. You'll be out of the gossip loop and you may just save them from causing a world of hurt.

> You know something is gossip when you're not part of the problem or part of the solution and you're talking about it.

Control your mouth! James is blunt in his

assessment of the tongue:

> *The tongue also is a fire, a world of evil among the parts of the body. It corrupts the whole person, sets the whole course of his life on fire, and is itself set on fire by hell. All kinds of animals, birds, reptiles and creatures of the sea are being tamed and have been tamed by man, but no man can tame the tongue. It is a restless evil, full of deadly poison. (James 3:6-9 NIV)*

James Goll has encouraged people to put an elastic band around their wrist and snap it whenever a negative or critical word comes from their mouth. It's a simple and powerful tool to train yourself to control your tongue. We have silicon bands available at 40DaysFromNegativity.com as a fun reminder for you. We like to suggest you pull them to stay positive in not only words, but thoughts and actions as well.

We All Stumble

If you ever catch yourself thinking condemning thoughts, being squeezed into a mould by a negative environment, excusing un-forgiveness, living offended at God, wallowing in discouragement, being judgmental, or gossiping, follow this 6-step plan:

1. Snap your band.
2. Stop it.
3. Repent.
4. Accept God's forgiveness.
5. Record it for your own records.
6. Talk about it with an accountability partner if you need encouragement.

Now these aren't all the answers to how to live "life above the negativity," but it's a start. In fact, if you can focus on one habit to change at a time, you'll have more success. Ask the Father what He'd like you to change and focus on that for the next 40 days.

If you're ready for a 40 day negativity fast, read the following pages, one day at a time. God bless you on your adventure. Don't forget, we have Bible Reading and Bible Memorization plans available at the back of this book.

from 10 minutes a day

LIFE ABOVE the Negativity

Day 1 -
Preparing for Battle

Truth:

> *Finally, be strong in the Lord and in his mighty power. Put on the full armor of God so that you can take your stand against the devil's schemes. For our struggle is not against flesh and blood, but against the rulers, against the authorities, against the powers of this dark world and against the spiritual forces of evil in the heavenly realms.*
> *Ephesians 6:10-12 (NIV)*

Thought:

When the children of Israel entered the promise land, it was to engage in battle with the enemies whose sin reached its full measure (Genesis 15:16). When they entered the land flowing with milk and honey, it wasn't a holiday. It wasn't time to relax. It was time to engage the enemy.

And the time for us to do the same is now.

Our enemy isn't flesh and blood and God is good so He hasn't called us to do something He hasn't already equipped us for.

God has provided us armor and "putting it on" is more than just saying, "I have put on the full armor of God!" Having the armor of God on is living out its implications for our lives.

Living with the armor of God in place is what we're going to be reminded of this first week as we refrain from any thought or talk that is contrary to the will of God expressed in Scripture.

Prayer:

> Lord, thank You for preparing us for every battle that we face. Thank You that You never leave us or forsake us. Thank You, You've called us your partners and co-workers and friends. Help us, Holy Spirit, to be overwhelmed with that once more.

Challenge:

We start by preparing ourselves to allow God to change us and a vocal declaration of truth opens the way for that to begin.

Just by saying, "I have put on the full armor of God!" doesn't mean we have... but it does mean we're willing. It's not a magic formula, but it has power to break down thoughts that set themselves up against the knowledge of God.

The challenge today should be easy for most, but some may find it a little silly or trite. Watch your judgmental attitude. When we're teachable, God can do miracles.

Today's challenge is to vocalize the declaration today and everyday this week we are reminded to have the full armor of God in place.

Then thank God for His Goodness in preparing you for every battle. Thank Him by faith if you can't see it in the moment.

LIFE ABOVE the Negativity

Declaration:

I choose to put on the full armor of God. I put on truth. I put on righteousness. I put on peace. I put on faith. I put on salvation. And I choose to learn to use the word of God with great power and in love.

Day 2 -
Be Real

Truth:

> *Again I say, don't get involved in foolish,*
> *ignorant arguments that only start fights.*
> *A servant of the Lord must not quarrel*
> *but must be kind to everyone, be able*
> *to teach, and be patient with difficult*
> *people.*
> > *2 Timothy 2:23-24 (NLT)*

Thought:

Paul is describing the uniform of a Roman Legionnaire in Ephesians 6. A soldier would be wearing a hanging tunic. It would have a belt around the middle to keep it flaps out-of-the-way and the outfit in place.

Derek Prince taught on the belt of truth that "We are to put away sham, clichés, religious hypocrisy, saying words that are just cop-outs and stop saying what we don't even believe. We can't just 'hang'."

We must be real. But real doesn't mean "fallen" - in Christ that's not who you are.

The Greek verb tenses in Ephesians 6:14, 15 is lost in the NIV, but trust me; it has three of the pieces of armor already on you. The belt, breastplate and shoes represent the parts of your protection you were given when you receive Jesus Christ. In them you are commanded to stand firm.

The Greek tense of the verb suggests the action it refers to was completed before we were commanded to stand firm. A Roman soldier would put on his belt, breastplate and shoes before trying to stand. In the same way, we are to put on the full armor of God after having already put on Christ. If you haven't made Jesus your Lord, this is meaningless.

But when you have made Jesus your Lord, we choose to live in truth and integrity. We should be in "place" with truth.

Are you?

Do you let your "yes" be "yes" and your "no", "no"? (James 5:12)

Do you keep your word, even when it hurts?

(Psalm 15:1-4)

Do you speak in love when you speak the truth? (Ephesians 4:15)

And you thought a fast from negativity was going to be an easy challenge.

Prayer:

Lord, I confess I have not always been a person of my word but I thank You, that with Your help, I can be starting now. Holy Spirit, convict me whenever I exaggerate even a little bit; tell me when I'm taking on more than I can honestly accomplish. Help me to keep my word, even when it hurts. I want people to know I'm happy to represent You.

Challenge:

Guard your conversation today and have integrity with who Christ has called you to be. You may need to confess exaggeration that makes you look better than you are or another one worse than they were.

Declaration:

I choose to put on the full armor of God. I put on truth. I put on righteousness. I put on peace. I put on faith. I put on salvation. And I choose to learn to use the word of God with great power and in love.

from 10 minutes a day

Day 3 -
Above All Else,
Guard Your Heart

Truth:

> Above all else, guard your heart, for it is
> the wellspring of life.
> Proverbs 4:23 (NIV)

Thought:

The breastplate protects the heart. The Breastplate of Righteousness described by Paul in Ephesians 6 is not from works gained from the Law (Philippians 3:9) but it is the righteousness of Christ we put on by faith (2 Corinthians 5:21). 1 Thessalonians uses the same motif of a breastplate and describes it as faith and love.

> But since we belong to the day, let us
> be self-controlled, putting on faith and
> love as a breastplate, and the hope of
> salvation as a helmet.
> 1 Thessalonians 5:8 (NIV)

Our own righteousness isn't going to cut it. In fact, if we work out of our own righteousness, satan can easily penetrate our breastplate and get to our heart. The breastplate of righteousness works in an active faith in Christ that works through love.

LIFE ABOVE the Negativity

Over this fast from negativity you're going to be reading much about love, because love is the antidote to negativity.

Love guards our heart. It protects what is most important. It reflects the nature of God.

The Breastplate of Righteousness protects our heart, which is the symbolic centre of our love. It's Christ's righteousness, which is His love shown to us. So as we accept His love and we respond to His love, we protect our capacity to love.

So are you ready to show Christ's love to others?

Prayer:

Lord, help me to put the needs of others ahead of my own. Help me to do everything in love. Empower me to live beyond my limited sphere of selfishness. Help me to love others because You first loved me.

Challenge:

Pray for opportunity to show God's love to someone today. Then respond to those you meet with love.

Declaration:

I choose to put on the full armor of God. I put on truth. I put on righteousness. I put on peace. I put on faith. I put on salvation. And I choose to learn to use the word of God with great power and in love.

from 10 minutes a day

Day 4 -
Are You Quick to See
God's Will Done?

Truth:

> *I pray that you may be active in sharing*
> *your faith, so that you will have a full*
> *understanding of every good thing we*
> *have in Christ.*
> *Philemon 1:6 (New International Version)*

Thought:

The shoes described in Ephesians 6 were strong, heavy sandals that were durable and provided mobility and availability to the commander. In our case, our commander is Jesus.

We need to be prepared to have an intelligent account of the Gospel. So many Christians don't even understand the basics of the Gospel. The kerygma (message) of Paul is straightforward –

> Jesus Christ has come in the flesh He died for our sins, was crucified, buried and raised from the dead, He ascended to heaven and will one day return to judge the living and the dead so repent!

It is a Gospel of Peace. We can only transfer peace to others if we have it ourselves. If we don't have peace then it's no use trying to give it to someone else. If you need peace, meditate on, and put into practice Isaiah 26:3, Romans 15:13 and Philippians 4:6-9.

Erwin McManus has an incredible story about a radio talk show host asking him: "So are everyone but Christians going to hell?"

He responded with something similar to, "Let me be up-front, I am a follower of Christ and know that He said He is the way to the Father. But He also didn't come into the world to condemn the world, so that's not something I can do either."

I enjoy Erwin's thinking because it's similar to my own. I was speaking to a Comparative Religions Class at a local university about the early church councils. It led beautifully into the question, "Is Jesus God?" I asked, "Have you ever been offended by someone telling you Jesus is the only way?" All but three were quick to agree.

I responded, "I'm a follower of Jesus and I ask you for forgiveness for others who name His name and use His words to condemn you. I'm sorry."

That got their attention, so I continued, "It would be perfectly legitimate to feel offended at Jesus, if He was just a man and He said, 'I am the way, the truth and the life.' But what if He was more than a man? What if He was the one who put 400 million stars in our galaxy and 400 million galaxies in our universe, and who knows how many more universes there are left to imagine? It would mean He wasn't being exclusive when He said He was the way, it would mean He was being inclusive, making a way where we couldn't make one on our own."

If the teacher wasn't a Muslim, I would have tried an altar call. People respond to a gospel of peace.

Having your shoes on means often doing for God

right there what He tells you to do. You obey without hesitation. You don't stall in communicating the Gospel of Peace in a way that meets people's needs right there and then.

Are you ready to put into practice the will of God expressed in Scripture?

Prayer:

Lord, I know You want me to be active in sharing my faith. I know You're not willing that any should perish. I know You will tell me what to say. I know You want my conversation full of grace seasoned with salt so I'll know how to answer everyone. Thank You, Holy Spirit, for empowering me to be Christ's witness. Empower me to make the most of every opportunity today to plant, water, or harvest Your word. I'll do it all for the glory of God.

Challenge:

Find someone to share the Gospel of Peace with today. Pray knowing its God's will for you to share your faith. Pray believing the Holy Spirit will teach you what to say. Then share your stories with us... Fast@40DaysFromNegativity.com

Declaration:

I choose to put on the full armor of God. I put on truth. I put on righteousness. I put on peace. I put on faith. I put on salvation. And I choose to learn to use the word of God with great power and in love.

Day 5 -
Testing Our Faith

from 10 minutes a day

Truth:

> *But if they had stood in my council,*
>   *they would have proclaimed my words*
> *to my people*
>   *and would have turned them from*
> *their evil ways*
>   *and from their evil deeds.*
> *Jeremiah 23:22 (NIV)*

Thought:

Without faith it's impossible to please God (Hebrews 11:6) because everything not done by faith is sin (Romans 14:23).

Faith is our obedient response to hearing the voice of God.

Faith is what protects us; it is our shield. The Roman shield covered everything the soldier was responsible for. So too our faith cover us. Faith is an excellent verb and a debilitating noun.

Faith comes by hearing and hearing by the present-spoken words of God (Romans 10:17).

How do we know what we're responsible for until we read it in the Bible or it's quickened in our Spirits?

What this means is we need to regularly have some quiet time with God. My brother-in-law coined my favorite term for it : "shut-up and listen time."

Jesus was pronounced "Immanuel" – God with us. We don't live in the 400 years before John, when God didn't speak to His people. We don't live in a time before Samuel when the word of God was rare. We are in a relationship with the One who spoke the worlds into being. Because of the blood of Christ we have direct access to the Father. Because of the Holy Spirit, we are empowered to communicate with God beyond our understanding. God still speaks to us today.

John 15:15 tells us that because we obey God, we are friends with Christ, no longer servants because servants don't we can know the plans of their Master. But Jesus lets us know what he learns from the Father.

Do we take the time to listen? When we listen, we can walk by faith. When we don't take time to listen, is it really faith we're walking in?

When you come before Him, quiet your Spirit, focus on His love and expect Him to speak, He does!

And He still speaks the words of life today (John 6:8). He speaks peace to the storms and there is fullness of joy in His presence. When we quiet ourselves and invite Him to speak, He will. When we're quick to obey – that's faith.

Test it and see.

Prayer:

Father, I come in the name of Jesus Christ with thanksgiving and praise and as I wait expectantly upon You now, I do my best to listen to Your voice. I stand before You, Almighty God and seek Your counsel. Please reveal any information I need; any strategies

*that I can employ right now so that I can
be knowing and doing what You want.*

Challenge:

Spend some "shut-up and listen time" (quiet time)
alone with God today. Finish up your requests and
leave time for Him to speak to you. Focus on His
love. Cease striving and rest. Expect Him to speak.
Some worshipful music can help. If you can't do it
for more than two minutes, take a scripture and think
about it from every possible angle with the love of
God in full view.

Declaration:

I choose to put on the full armor of God. I put on
truth. I put on righteousness. I put on peace. I put on
faith. I put on salvation. And I choose to learn to use
the word of God with great power and in love.

Day 6 -
Hope that is Real

Truth:

> *But since we belong to the day, let us*
> *be self-controlled, putting on faith and*
> *love as a breastplate, and the hope of*
> *salvation as a helmet.*
> *1 Thessalonians 5:8 (NIV)*

Thought:

The helmet of salvation protects our mind and 1 Thessalonians 5:8 tells us our mind represents hope. Faith is the substance of things hoped for (Hebrews 11:1) and so real hope can only be built on faith.

Hope is a quiet expectation of the fulfillment of God's promises. In a sense it is continuous optimism. Hope that is built on faith and negativity can't exist together.

If we believe Romans 8:28, then there is no reason for pessimism, self-pity, doubt, or mistrust ...we are saved by hope.

Hopelessness is the condition of those away from God. It should never be the condition of the Christian because "Christ in us is the hope of glory" (Colossians 1:27).

Hope is an essential part of our Salvation experience. When we have Hope, we are anchored. Hope is optimism.

Hope needs to be seen and so it requires some

response to the faith on which it is built. Are you trusting God to be true to His word? Take Psalm 34:19 as an example:

> The righteous person faces many
> troubles, but the Lord comes to the
> rescue each time.

Are you needing Him to come to the rescue? Then respond to each promise in scripture with praise. It shows the hope that you have.

Prayer:

> Lord, I am so thankful it is not my
> righteousness that allows me to stand before
> You and be called Your child. It is Your
> righteousness that makes me right in the
> Father's eyes. Thank You Lord, I have never
> seen the righteous forsaken or the children
> of the righteous begging for bread. Thank
> You for being our provider. Thank you for
> You own the cattle on a thousand hills. You
> are Good and don't give Your children a
> serpent when we need a fish, or a rock
> when we need bread. Thank You for being
> trustworthy. Thank You for being worthy.

Challenge:

Take some time today to praise God no matter your situation. Praise Him especially if you don't feel like it. Praise Him for who He is. Praise Him for what He's done. Praise Him for what He's promised.

Declaration:

I choose to put on the full armor of God. I put on truth. I put on righteousness. I put on peace. I put on faith. I put on salvation. And I choose to learn to use the word of God with great power and in love.

Day 7 -
When Worry Isn't Negative

Truth:

> *Your word is a lamp to my feet*
> *and a light for my path.*
> *I have taken an oath and confirmed it,*
> *that I will follow your righteous laws.*
> *Psalm 119:105-106 (NIV)*

Thought:

The sword of the Spirit is the main offensive weapon mentioned in Ephesians 6 – prayer is another. Lies we believe can't stand up to the word of God.

When satan tempted Jesus in the desert, Jesus always responded to the half truth with the full truth from the word of God. He didn't argue points – he pointed out Scripture.

We need to do the same. To do it effectively we need to have the word of God inside of us. We can't be passive in our knowledge, memorization and meditation of scripture. It's our bread; our life.

Now, most of us who have been on the journey for a while know we can always learn more from the Bible and we should know the benefits of putting it to memory, but when the Bible says "I meditate..." how do we do that?

If you know how to worry, you know how to meditate. It's like a cow chewing its cud. You think about a passage 100 different ways. You go over it

from 10 minutes a day

LIFE ABOVE the Negativity

again and again and again and again. It starts to work its way into your being and brings faith with it. It's much like how worry brings fear into your being. Worry is negative because it grows fear. Meditation is positive because it grows faith.

Prayer:

Thank you, Lord, for Your word that is able to teach, rebuke, correct and train in righteousness. It is my bread. It is life. Thank You that by it I know about Your love, creation, friendship, salvation, mercy, grace, peace, assurance, restoration, cleansing, power, wisdom and knowledge. Thank You, Your word is alive and reads me. Speak to me as I read it. May I only read to learn more about You.

Challenge:

Pick a passage and meditate on it today. Spend some time in the morning; think about it throughout the day. Consider it on your bed at night. You'll be living the command in Philippians 4:8:

And now, dear brothers and sisters, one final thing. Fix your thoughts on what is true, and honorable, and right, and pure, and lovely, and admirable. Think about things that are excellent and worthy of praise. (NLT)

Declaration:

I choose to put on the full armor of God. I put on truth. I put on righteousness. I put on peace. I put on faith. I put on salvation. And I choose to learn to use the word of God with great power and in love.

from 10 minutes a day

Day 8 -
Fruit Happens

Truth:

> *You were taught, with regard to your former way of life, to put off your old self, which is being corrupted by its deceitful desires; to be made new in the attitude of your minds; and to put on the new self, created to be like God in true righteousness and holiness.*
> *Ephesians 4:22-24 (NIV)*

Thought:

The Bible is so rich with metaphors that we can see in the natural. When you think about it, how else could the created understand the Creator? We recognize our language and experience is limited by our mortality, but at the same time we realize it is God who has revealed Himself to us.

That thought alone makes me stop and worship. I wish I could relay it more profoundly.

Here's one that makes me go "Ah ha!"

> The moon does not have its own light, but reflects the light of the sun to the part of the world that's away from the light. There are two things that happen to stop the light from the sun being reflected to the world. They both have to do with the position of the moon.

LIFE ABOVE the Negativity

1. When the world comes between the moon and sun- whose light it was created to reflect to the part of the world that's away from the sun- it's called a lunar eclipse. The shadow of the world covers the face of the moon that reflects the light of the sun.

2. The moon is also able to come between the sun and the side of the world that is directly receiving its light. The shadow of the moon covers a portion of the earth instead of reflecting the sun's light to the side of the world that is away from the sun. We call that a solar eclipse.

However, there is also a time when the moon is in the perfect position to reflect the greatest amount of the light of the sun, to the part of the world that is away from the sun. It is the brightest, biggest moon of the year and it happens in the Northern Hemisphere in the Fall. We happen to call that the "harvest moon."

The same is true for us. We reflect the goodness of God by choosing to grow the fruit of Spirit that reflects His good nature. It puts us in the position to reflect the greatest amount of His light to the part of the world that is still in darkness.

Love, joy, peace, patience, kindness, goodness, faithfulness, gentleness and self-control together show the nature of Jesus to the world. And there are two truths about fruit we need to be aware of.

The first is – Fruit happens. Jesus is the vine; we are the branches. When we abide in Him, we bear much fruit. It's as natural as the moon reflecting the light from the sun to the side of the world that's away from the sun. The lesson is abiding in the vine.

The second truth is – we need to tend an orchard. This thought doesn't contradict the first, although I admit I'm mixing metaphors. Growing in the fruit of the Spirit is a choice we make, as well as a series of choices throughout the day. We will constantly need to choose love, joy, peace and patience. We will have opportunity to choose kindness, goodness and faithfulness. Conditions will be conducive for us to not wish to choose gentleness and self-control.

So does fruit just happen, or do we tend the tree? Both. Learn how to abide and fruit just happens. Abiding means keeping in step with the rhythms of the Master and in our fallen state it is a choice to reflect the light of the sun to the side of the world that's away from the sun.

The next few days we'll be encouraged to make that choice a habit.

Prayer:

Thank you, Lord, that when I abide in You, Your words abide in me and I can ask whatever I want and it will be given to me. Teach me to abide. Thank You, Holy Spirit, You will empower me to put on and grow love, joy, peace, patience, kindness, goodness, faithfulness, gentleness and self-control.

Challenge:

If you could show God to the world in any way that reflects His goodness and Glory, how would you do it? Pray and obey. There are things you can do today that will see that prayer fulfilled. Do them.

Declaration:

I choose to reflect the light of the Son to the side of the world that's away from the Son. I choose to put on love, joy, peace, patience, kindness, goodness, faithfulness, gentleness and self-control.

from 10 minutes a day

Day 9 -
The Antidote to Negativity

Truth:

> *Love is patient, love is kind. It does not*
> *envy, it does not boast, it is not proud.*
> *It is not rude, it is not self-seeking, it is*
> *not easily angered, it keeps no record of*
> *wrongs. Love does not delight in evil but*
> *rejoices with the truth. It always protects,*
> *always trusts, always hopes, always*
> *perseveres. Love never fails.*
> *1 Corinthians 13:4-8 (NIV)*

Thought:

Love is the antidote to negativity. How can you act in love and speak:

Careless words   Matthew 12:35-37, (HCSB)

"Loose" words   Proverbs 10:19, (NIV)

Angry words   James 1:19, (NLT)

Cutting words   Proverbs 12:18, (NLT)

Discouraging words Numbers 32:7, (NIV)

Untruthful words Ephesians 4:25, (NIV)

Complaining words Phil. 2:14-16,(NLT)
Slanderous words Eph. 4:31, (NIV)

Obscene words Ephesians 5:4, (NIV)
Abusive Words Ephesians 4:29, (NLT)

Dissenting Words Proverbs 16:28, (NIV)

Or Gossip? Proverbs 20:19 (NLT)

You can't.

LIFE ABOVE the Negativity

Love fulfills the law (Romans 13:10). It is the revealed nature of God (1 John 4:16). It is how we are to treat one another (John 13:34-35). It's how we are to behave towards everyone (Luke 10:27).

Yet the word "love" is trite. It's not specific enough. We love our spouse. We love our dog. We love jalapeños in sandwiches. How can we know what love is?

We need to understand love the way God wants us to understand it. We can only define our love by how God loved us:

> This is love: not that we loved God, but that he loved us and sent his Son as an atoning sacrifice for our sins. 1 John 4:10 (New International Version)

> Husbands, go all out in your love for your wives, exactly as Christ did for the church—a love marked by giving, not getting. Christ's love makes the church whole. His words evoke her beauty. Everything he does and says is designed to bring the best out of her, dressing her in dazzling white silk, radiant with holiness. And that is how husbands ought to love their wives. They're really doing themselves a favor—since they're already "one" in marriage. Ephesians 5:25-28 (The Message)

And we can only measure our love, by the way God measures it:

This is how we know that we love the children of God: by loving God and carrying out his commands. This is love for God: to obey his commands. And his commands are not burdensome, for everyone born of God overcomes the world. This is the victory that has overcome the world, even our faith. 1 John 5:2-4 (New International Version)

So "love" means obedience to God. Love means self-sacrifice. Love means you show it before the other one deserves it.

Have you shown that love to someone today?

Prayer:

Lord, I thank You that Your commands are not burdensome and I thank You You've given the Holy Spirit to help me in my weakness. I want to reflect Your goodness to people not directly in Your light. Help me show love even before I feel like it, so the love I show can be sincere. Thank You that since this prayer is according to Your will, I know I have what I ask of You.

Challenge:

Every time you speak careless, "loose," angry, cutting, discouraging, untruthful, complaining, slanderous, obscene, abusive or dissenting words and gossip, confess it to God and ask the forgiveness of the one you spoke them to. Have grace for others who speak them to you.

Declaration:

I choose to reflect the light of the Son to the side of the world that's away from the Son. I choose to put on love, joy, peace, patience, kindness, goodness, faithfulness, gentleness and self-control.

from 10 minutes a day

Day 10 -
Our Strength is No Secret

Truth:

> *This day is sacred to our Lord. Do not grieve, for the joy of the LORD is your strength. Nehemiah 8:10 (New International Version)*

Thought:

The book of Nehemiah is such a good analogy for our fast from negativity. If I would have seen it early enough, the 40 day fast from negativity would have been 52 days, since that's how long it took the people to re-build the walls of Jerusalem to a defensible position and that's a metaphor for what we're doing now.

Those rebuilding the walls endured distraction, ridicule and discouragement. This is what most of us have endured as we rid ourselves of everything contrary to the will of God expressed in Scripture.

Negativity saps our joy, but Nehemiah told the people to stop looking at the situation because "the joy of the Lord is your strength."

Joy, like all of the fruit of the Spirit, is a choice. It's something we choose to have despite our situation. Now that's not very practical or encouraging when you're in the middle of disappointment and discouragement. So here's another truth that is more practical:

Joy is something we choose to pursue. David wrote:

> You have made known to me the path
> of life; you will fill me with joy in your
> presence, with eternal pleasures at your
> right hand.
> Psalm 16:11 (NIV)

We can practice the presence of God and recognize He is everywhere present and find joy in knowing that. We also need to pursue the palpable presence of God, slowing our conversation with Him and taking time to listen to His voice.

And joy can overwhelm us, regardless of the circumstance we face.

Prayer:

> Lord, I need joy. I need laughter. I need to
> celebrate the good things that a good God
> has given me and made for me. Lord, You are
> good and You fill me with joy in your presence.
> Help me to recognize Your presence today.
> Fill me with joy as I make time to pursue Your
> palpable presence. Your joy is my strength.

Challenge:

Choose joy today. Practice the presence of God – slow down enough to recognize He is everywhere present. Pursue the palpable presence of God - spend some time relaxing in His presence, expecting Him to fill you with joy.

from 10 minutes a day

LIFE ABOVE the Negativity

Declaration:

I choose to reflect the light of the Son to the side of the world that's away from the sun. I choose to put on love, joy, peace, patience, kindness, goodness, faithfulness, gentleness and self-control.

Day 11 -
<u>Seek Peace and Pursue it</u>

Truth:

> *You will keep in perfect peace*
> *all who trust in you,*
> *all whose thoughts are fixed on you!*
> *Isaiah 26:3 (New Living Translation)*

Thought:

When we were in New Zealand, everyone was so laid-back compared with what we were used to in North America. When you signaled to change lanes on a busy motorway, people would actually give way to you. It was astounding.

Few were in a hurry. "No worries" is the standard reply. No one seemed busy... unless you were in the church.

I spoke to some of my pastor friends about this: "How can you reach a culture that's laid-back, when you seem to take pride in being busy?" I suppose what I meant was, how can the church teach peace when they don't experience it?

I'm not pointing fingers here. In North America it's so much worse. We add church programs into a busy schedule and feel holiest when we are close to burnout. How can we have "feet fitted with the gospel of peace" when we don't have peace?

But we can have peace. It's our choice to obey God.

We can fix our thoughts on Him (Isaiah 26:3) and

take all of our requests to Him with thanksgiving (Philippians 4:6-8). We can forgive others for our sake and choose to live un-offended at God. We can cease striving and give up our right to understand so we can have the peace that passes understanding.

So will you?

Prayer:

> *Lord, in my weakness You are strong and I need Your strength to help me choose peace. I need Your peace to share Your good news. I need Your peace to calm me in the storm. I need Your peace so others will see Your goodness and greatness in me. I choose today to seek peace and pursue it.*

Challenge:

Take everything you are worrying about and thank God for the answers that are promised in His word. Meditate on Matthew 6:7-34.

Declaration:

I choose to reflect the light of the Son to the side of the world that's away from the Son. I choose to put on love, joy, peace, patience, kindness, goodness, faithfulness, gentleness and self-control.

Day 12 -
Is Patience Inaction?

Truth:

Dear brothers and sisters, when troubles come your way, consider it an opportunity for great joy. For you know that when your faith is tested, your endurance has a chance to grow. So let it grow, for when your endurance is fully developed, you will be perfect and complete, needing nothing. James 1:2-4 (New Living Translation)

Thought:

Is patience the same as inaction?

Patience is releasing your will so God's will can be done through you. God's will has moments of sitting still – Jesus always spent time alone with God. When we choose to do the same... to discipline ourselves to sit still longer than fifteen minutes... we learn to move to the rhythms of His grace.

His rhythm seldom means inaction. Even when we wait on God, we must choose to wait with expectation. We know He's good and is the giver of good gifts. We know He won't give His children a stone when they ask for bread, or a serpent when they ask for a fish.

Patience becomes real when our timetables get set aside for God's timetable. If God wasn't patient with us – not wanting for any to perish – none of us would be here.

from 10 minutes a day

It's His patience with us that we need to reflect to the part of the world that is away from the Son.

How do we do that?

We show love. Remember, it's the antidote to negativity. Love is patient. It is kind. It reflects who God is – as do all the fruit of the Spirit we're growing in our lives.

Don't worry, if not today, soon, you will have opportunity for your faith to be tested to produce even more patience. Today you'll need to choose to be patient with others, and so doing, show God's love to them.

Prayer:

Lord I know that You are patient with me and I know I haven't been patient with (insert the names). Thank You that You'll help me become more like You. Thank You that You're helping me to show Your love to others. I choose to be patient today and always. Help me to be patient to bring glory to You.

Challenge:

Go the speed limit today. Stop at all red lights. Change your schedule so that you're not in a rush. Slow down and show patience for others.

Declaration:

I choose to reflect the light of the Son to the side of the world that's away from the Son. I choose to put on love, joy, peace, patience, kindness, goodness, faithfulness, gentleness and self-control.

Day 13 -
Kindness Rules

Truth:

> But I say, love your enemies! Pray for
> those who persecute you! In that way,
> you will be acting as true children of
> your Father in heaven. For he gives his
> sunlight to both the evil and the good,
> and he sends rain on the just and the
> unjust alike. If you love only those who
> love you, what reward is there for that?
> Even corrupt tax collectors do that much.
> If you are kind only to your friends, how
> are you different from anyone else? Even
> pagans do that. But you are to be perfect,
> even as your Father in heaven is perfect.
> Matthew 5:44-48 (New Living
> Translation)

Thought:

Can you remember the last time someone showed you kindness ...when it wasn't to repay something you did for him or her, or to sell you something, or even to make an impression?

Doesn't it just encourage you to remember someone like that?

Those are the people I like to hang around. They are the ones I need to learn from.

Of course, most have learned it from God. Did you know God enjoys showing kindness towards all He has made?

...but let him who boasts boast about this: that he understands and knows me, that I am the LORD, who exercises kindness, justice and righteousness on earth, for in these I delight," declares the LORD. Jeremiah 9:24 (New International Version)

Did you know there are results when we don't respond to His kindness?

About that time Hezekiah became deathly ill. He prayed to the Lord, who healed him and gave him a miraculous sign. But Hezekiah did not respond appropriately to the kindness shown him, and he became proud. So the Lord's anger came against him and against Judah and Jerusalem. 2 Chronicles 32:24-25 (New Living Translation)

Did you know God alone can respond the way He did against Hezekiah?

Do not take revenge, my friends, but leave room for God's wrath, for it is written: "It is mine to avenge; I will repay," says the Lord. Romans 12:19 (New International Version)

God's justice is for God alone to wield. Jesus wants

us to leave everything in God's hands and to reflect the nature of God to those who can't pay us back.

> Then Jesus said to his host, "When you give a luncheon or dinner, do not invite your friends, your brothers or relatives, or your rich neighbors; if you do, they may invite you back and so you will be repaid. But when you give a banquet, invite the poor, the crippled, the lame, the blind, and you will be blessed. Although they cannot repay you, you will be repaid at the resurrection of the righteous."
> Luke 14:12-14
> (New International Version)

Can we be kind and expect nothing in return? Can we obey what Jesus said in Luke 6:35 and show kindness to even those who consider us enemies?

You can because the nature of God is written and being rewritten on the parchment of your heart. You are shining His light to the side of the world that's away from the Son. And He empowers you to do it:

1. Because of God
2. With Jesus
3. Empowered by the Holy Spirit

These are the Kindness Rules to allow kindness to rule.

from 10 minutes a day

LIFE ABOVE the Negativity

Prayer:

> *Lord, thank You for showing me kindness
> and help me to respond to it by showing it
> to others. I don't want this to be a program
> I try for a certain number of days. I need
> this to be the pattern for my life. Help me to
> show kindness to all – to those close, to those
> against, and to those who cannot repay. Show
> me who I can show Your kindness to today
> and how I can do it so You get the glory.*

Challenge:

There's someone that has come to your mind that you need to be kind to today. It could be a neighbor, a co-worker, an extended family member, a person on the bus or a stranger on the street. Show them kindness that isn't owed them, and don't do it to have kindness returned. Send us your stories - fast@40Day sFromNegativity.com.

Declaration:

I choose to reflect the light of the Son to the side of the world that's away from the Son. I choose to put on love, joy, peace, patience, kindness, goodness, faithfulness, gentleness and self-control.

Day 14 -
It's Good to Do Good

Truth:

> How can I repay the LORD
> for all his goodness to me? Psalm
> 116:12 (New International Version)

Thought:

I don't consider myself a modern thinker. I'm resistant to the labels others try to force on me. I think about webs of relationships, not linear cause-and-effect. I can hold multiple conflicting thoughts without any angst. And I'm a follower of Christ.

I know this makes some people nervous. However, I'm believing that from post-post-modernity the greatest theologians in history will emerge.

I do have a problem with the way many people, especially those with my thinking process, carry out truth. We can believe something is true, but it doesn't make a difference in our lives. Truth doesn't matter if we don't work out its implication into our lives. If it doesn't matter, can it be true?

Let me give you an example.

Ask anyone to create a scale of goodness. Pick a spot on the wall – the top is good, the bottom is bad. Tell them to choose an example for the bottom – it'll be someone like Hitler. Ask them to have an example for the top – Mother Teresa will usually come up. Ask them where they think the average person in the

from 10 minutes a day

LIFE ABOVE the Negativity

world is on the continuum and depending on their view of life, the average will be anywhere from the middle of the scale or slightly below, up to halfway or to the top or slightly more.

Now, ask them to say where they are. We inevitably say we're better than the average. (If you don't think you are, you may have some issues with guilt. Read 1 John 1:9, then repent and know you're forgiven.)

How can we all be better than average?

It is because we judge ourselves by our intent and judge everyone else by their actions.

Sorry news… the Bible tells us to judge goodness by what we do. Intentions are not good enough. It's not "being good' that is important, it's "doing good" that counts with God.

Finally, all of you should be of one mind. Sympathize with each other. Love each other as brothers and sisters. Be tenderhearted, and keep a humble attitude. Don't repay evil for evil. Don't retaliate with insults when people insult you. Instead, pay them back with a blessing. That is what God has called you to do, and he will bless you for it. For the Scriptures say,

*"If you want to enjoy life
   and see many happy days,
keep your tongue from speaking evil
   and your lips from telling lies.
Turn away from evil and do good.
   Search for peace, and work to
maintain it.
The eyes of the Lord watch over those*

who do right,
    and his ears are open to their prayers.
    But the Lord turns his face
        against those who do evil." 1 Peter
3:8-13 (New Living Translation)

So as we intentionally grow the fruit of goodness, we need to do "good". We don't need to feel "good". We don't need to think "good". We need to *do* "good".

And you already know what "good" is because you belong to the One who is Good.

Do to others as you would have them do
to you.
Luke 6:31 (NIV)

Who will you show goodness to today?

Prayer:

Lord, thank You for creating me the way I
am. Thank You I was born for this time and
created for eternity. Thank You so much for
the goodness You've shown me. Thank You for
Your forgiveness and mercy and provision and
blessing. Empower me, Holy Spirit, to show
that same goodness to someone today.

from 10 minutes a day

LIFE ABOVE the Negativity

Challenge:

Treat everyone today, the way you would want to be treated. That includes the telemarketer that calls during supper and the unenlightened individual that cuts you off in traffic while he or she was talking on there mobile. Make it a habit… who knows where it could lead?

Declaration:

I choose to reflect the light of the Son to the side of the world that's away from the Son. I choose to put on love, joy, peace, patience, kindness, goodness, faithfulness, gentleness and self-control.

Day 15 -
Godly Tenacity Over Time

from 10 minutes a day

Truth:

If you are faithful in little things, you will be faithful in large ones. But if you are dishonest in little things, you won't be honest with greater responsibilities.
Luke 16:10 (New Living Translation)

Thought:

How long does it take for a mountain to rise from the sea? How long does it take for the rivers to take the stone back to the ocean depths? How long will it be before there is more usable beachfront on the Hawaiian Islands... and is it too early to invest?

Have you noticed God thinks generationally? He's the God of Abraham, Isaac and Jacob. Yet we tend to think in terms of yesterday... and maybe tomorrow. No wonder faithfulness is such an obscure idea for many of our minds to grasp.

Faithfulness is Godly tenacity over time.

Should we dissect that a bit? "Godly" means it is in line or obedient to the will of God. "Tenacity" is simply stick-to-it-ness. And over time means it's not for a moment.

So can we define what God wants us to be faithful in? There are a few thoughts in scripture that focus on the need for our faithfulness.

Be True To Your Word

Just say a simple, 'Yes, I will,' or 'No, I won't.' Anything beyond this is from the evil one. Matthew 5:37 (New Living Translation)

Honor Your Marriage

Give honor to marriage, and remain faithful to one another in marriage. God will surely judge people who are immoral and those who commit adultery. Hebrews 13:4 (New Living Translation)

Use Your Talents

God has given each of you a gift from his great variety of spiritual gifts. Use them well to serve one another. 1 Peter 4:10 (New Living Translation)

Guard Your Tongue

And the tongue is a flame of fire. It is a whole world of wickedness, corrupting your entire body. It can set your whole life on fire, for it is set on fire by hell itself. People can tame all kinds of animals, birds, reptiles, and fish, but no one can tame the tongue. It is restless and evil, full of deadly poison. Sometimes it praises our Lord and Father, and sometimes it

*curses those who have been made in
the image of God. And so blessing and
cursing come pouring out of the same
mouth. Surely, my brothers and sisters,
this is not right! James 3:6-10 (New Living
Translation)*

Manage Your Money

*And if you are untrustworthy about
worldly wealth, who will trust you with
the true riches of heaven? Luke 16:11
(New Living Translation)*

Be Committed To Your Local Church

*Be devoted to one another in brotherly
love. Honor one another above
yourselves. Never be lacking in zeal,
but keep your spiritual fervor, serving
the Lord. Romans 12:10-11 (New
International Version)*

We can't do these things for a season and consider ourselves to be faithful. You can't honor your marriage until times get tough. You can't use your talent until your interest wanes. You can't manage your money well just until there is a good sale.

You can't be a little bit pregnant and you can't be a little bit faithful. You either are or you are not.

The great news is God is faithful. 2 Timothy 2:13 says: "If we are faithless, He remains faithful; for He cannot deny Himself." Because He's faithful we can have faith in Him to finish what He's started. Philippians 1:6 says: "he who began a good work in you will carry it on to completion until the day of Christ Jesus."

So if today is the day you start having godly tenacity over time, then great. Welcome. None of us can ever say "I've arrived." But it's wonderful to have one more on the journey.

God is going to bless you for it:

> He grants a treasure of common sense to the honest.
> He is a shield to those who walk with integrity.
> He guards the paths of the just
> and protects those who are faithful to him.
> Proverbs 2:7-8 (New Living Translation)

Prayer:

> Lord, I haven't always been faithful. I confess my sin and ask You to forgive me. Thank You that Your word says when I confess my sins You are faithful and just to forgive me of those sins and to clean me from all unrighteousness. I want to be faithful because I want to reflect Your faithfulness to those who can only see You through me.

Challenge:

Are you faithfully managing everything that God has entrusted to you? Is there one of the areas above that you are struggling in? Confess it to a friend and to God and ask them to hold you accountable to be faithful.

Declaration:

I choose to reflect the light of the Son to the side of the world that's away from the Son. I choose to put on love, joy, peace, patience, kindness, goodness, faithfulness, gentleness and self-control.

from 10 minutes a day

Day 16 -
Is Meekness Weakness?

Truth:

> *Let your gentleness be evident to all. The*
> *Lord is near.*
> *Philippians 4:5 (NIV)*

Thought:

Mothers like to label their sons as "gentle." I've never seen a son respond well to that label. I somehow remember starting a fight with someone just to prove I wasn't "gentle." How's that for a fallen nature?

Gentleness is an expression of compassion seen as God deals with the frail and weak and it's also His expectation for how His followers should treat one another. He is the sun, we are the moon. We reflect the light of the sun to the side of the world that's away from its direct glory.

We're told to be gentle with everyone:

> *Remind the believers to submit to the*
> *government and its officers. They should*
> *be obedient, always ready to do what*
> *is good. They must not slander anyone*
> *and must avoid quarreling. Instead, they*
> *should be gentle and show true humility*
> *to everyone.*
> *Titus 3:1-2 (NLT)*

But specifically we're to be gentle with others in the following circumstances:

Correcting The Wayward

> *Dear brothers and sisters, if another believer is overcome by some sin, you who are godly should gently and humbly help that person back onto the right path. And be careful not to fall into the same temptation yourself.*
> *Galatians 6:1 (NLT)*

> *A servant of the Lord must not quarrel but must be kind to everyone, be able to teach, and be patient with difficult people. Gently instruct those who oppose the truth. Perhaps God will change those people's hearts, and they will learn the truth.*
> *2 Timothy 2:24-25 (NLT)*

Reasoning with pre-Christians

> *Instead, you must worship Christ as Lord of your life. And if someone asks about your Christian hope, always be ready to explain it. But do this in a gentle and respectful way. Keep your conscience clear. Then if people speak against you, they will be ashamed when they see what a good life you live because you belong to Christ.*
> *1 Peter 3:15-16 (NLT)*

from 10 minutes a day

Nurturing the newly planted

As apostles of Christ we could have been a burden to you, but we were gentle among you, like a mother caring for her little children. 1 Thessalonians 2:7 (New International Version)

Jesus was meek, but He wasn't weak. He didn't need to exert His authority, He moved in His authority. We're to be like Christ in this world. We don't need to defend ourselves, we don't need to force others to see things the same way we do. I absolutely enjoy how Eugene Peterson gets this sentiment across.

Since this is the kind of life we have chosen, the life of the Spirit, let us make sure that we do not just hold it as an idea in our heads or a sentiment in our hearts, but work out its implications in every detail of our lives. That means we will not compare ourselves with each other as if one of us were better and another worse. We have far more interesting things to do with our lives. Each of us is an original. Live creatively, friends. Galatians 5:25-6:1a(The Message)

When you look to Christ, it's hard to judge someone else with anything but gentleness. We need to choose to be gentle.

Prayer:

Lord, if I have shown distain for gentleness, I confess it as sin and ask for Your forgiveness. Help me to be like Christ who would not break a bruised reed or snuff out a smoldering wick. Give me Your mind to know how to react in every situation. Empower me to be gentle to everyone.

Challenge:

A soft answer turns away wrath. The next time you have opportunity to be harsh, choose to be gentle.

Declaration:

I choose to reflect the light of the Son to the side of the world that's away from the Son. I choose to put on love, joy, peace, patience, kindness, goodness, faithfulness, gentleness and self-control.

from 10 minutes a day

Day 17 -
Savoring Self-Control

Truth:

> *So think clearly and exercise self-control.*
> *Look forward to the gracious salvation*
> *that will come to you when Jesus Christ is*
> *revealed to the world.*
> *1 Peter 1:13 (NLT)*

Thought:

Self-control is a mark of wisdom. Proverbs 29:11 says, "A fool gives full vent to his anger, but a wise man keeps himself under control" (NIV). Self-control is one of the most difficult fruit to grow for some people.

Our culture tells us to, "Buy now, pay later." We move out of our parent's home and want to get everything they took a lifetime to gather, in just a couple of years. We're taught to have an attention span of 6 minutes – until the next commercial. We're trained to expect instant gratification.

So is there any hope to grow the fruit of self-control?

With God there always is hope. It's so much easier to be self-controlled when you let the Spirit control you.

Here's an example: I've tried different times to diet and lose some weight. I don't have the self-control to stick to it. But my wife and I felt led by God to do an extended Daniel fast. We abstained from everything but vegetables, fruit, water, whole grains and nuts. I was doing it in obedience to God and unto him. I knew it was His will and that He would help me do His will. I wasn't trying to lose weight, but I did.

So it's good to know His will and that He helps us to do His will.

It's His will for us to control our bodies:

> God's will is for you to be holy, so stay away from all sexual sin. Then each of you will control his own body and live in holiness and honor— not in lustful passion like the pagans who do not know God and his ways. Never harm or cheat a Christian brother in this matter by violating his wife, for the Lord avenges all such sins, as we have solemnly warned you before. God has called us to live holy lives, not impure lives.
> 1 Thessalonians 4:3-7 (NLT)

It's His will for us to control our minds:

> The end of all things is near. Therefore be clear minded and self-controlled so that you can pray.
> 1 Peter 4:7 (NIV)

It's His will for us to control our mouths:

> Watch your tongue and keep your mouth shut, and you will stay out of trouble.
> Proverbs 21:23 (NLT)

from 10 minutes a day

And He's given us the Holy Spirit to teach and empower us to live self-controlled lives:

> *For the grace of God that brings salvation has appeared to all men. It teaches us to say "No" to ungodliness and worldly passions, and to live self-controlled, upright and godly lives in this present age,*
> *Titus 2:11-12 (NIV)*

Isn't God good?

Prayer:

> *Lord, I need Your help to grow self-control. I know it's not my determination that makes me right before You. It's Your grace and mercy that I need to grow this fruit. Empower me to control my body, my thoughts and my mouth...all for Your glory.*

Challenge:

Do you need to grow self-control in an area of your life? Confess it to God, ask Him to help you, and then find someone today to help you stay accountable.

Declaration:

I choose to reflect the light of the Son to the side of the world that's away from the Son. I choose to put on love, joy, peace, patience, kindness, goodness, faithfulness, gentleness and self-control.

Day 18 -
Replacing Lies with the Truth

Truth:

> You will show me the way of life,
> granting me the joy of your presence
> and the pleasures of living with you
> forever.
> Psalm 16:11 (New Living Translation)

Thought:

Many have lies they choose to believe. These lies come in to help us "heal" wounds that we've been afflicted with. It's not actual healing that occurs; it's a snare of the enemy to gain a stronghold in our lives.

Try this exercise:

1. List 10 words of affirmation that have stuck with you since you first heard them.

2. Now list 10 words of death that have stuck with you since you first heard them.

3. Which list was easier to recall?

4. Which list had more emotional triggers?

Living in a fallen world, and living with fallen

from 10 minutes a day

people, we've all been wounded. Lies are what others have told us in our past. They may not have been spoken to us directly, but we've internalized them nonetheless. They are deceitful, downgrading and condemning.

For example:

"I can't do it."

"I'm worthless."

"I'm stupid."

"I'm ugly."

"I'm useless."

They are so much a part of us that until we can see the lies, we won't know we have them. We won't know to see them, until we know who we are in Christ.

In Christ, there is now no more condemnation (Romans 8:1) so we know the thoughts that we are condemned with are not His.

The power of God can set you free from the chains of condemnation. This is your part to play:

> For though we live in the world, we
> do not wage war as the world does.
> The weapons we fight with are not the
> weapons of the world. On the contrary,
> they have divine power to demolish
> strongholds. We demolish arguments and
> every pretension that sets itself up against
> the knowledge of God, and we take
> captive every thought to make it obedient
> to Christ.
> 2 Corinthians 10:3-5 (NIV)

You heal the wounds the lies have sought to cover up by choosing to believe and live out of the truth. Over the next few days we'll focus on four areas where many followers of Christ cling to lies. What we want to do is transform our thinking so we won't be squeezed into the mold of the world.

> *"Don't let the world around you squeeze you into its own mold, but let God remold your minds from within, so that you may prove in practice that the plan of God for you is good, meets all his demands, and moves toward the goal of true maturity"* (Romans 12:1-3; Phillips)

We don't have time to cover all the areas where Christians may have strongholds in their thinking. But we don't want you to be unprepared.

Go to 40DaysFromNegativity.com and click on the logo on the top left-hand column. You're able to print off a personalized "Identity in Christ" as well as your name in the book of Ephesians. These are wonderful tools to help you know the truth about how God sees you.

Choose to replace the lies with the truth.

LIFE ABOVE the Negativity

Prayer:

Lord, show me the areas where I believe lies. Forgive me of them and remold my thinking with the truth of how You see me. I will fill my mind with Your thoughts and allow healing to take place in my wounded-ness.

Challenge:

Go to 40DaysFromNegativity.com and print off your personalized "Identity in Christ". Read the truths out loud. Pray them with authority; knowing it's how God sees you.

Declaration:

I choose to believe what God says about me. I choose to live out of what I choose to believe. I choose to replace the lies that have attached themselves to wounds from my past with the truth of how God sees my situation and me.

Day 19 -
I Am Valuable

Truth:

> But now, God's Message, the God who
> made you in the first place, Jacob,
>   the One who got you started, Israel:
> "Don't be afraid, I've redeemed you.
>   I've called your name. You're mine.
> When you're in over your head, I'll be
> there with you.
>   When you're in rough waters, you will
> not go down.
> When you're between a rock and a hard
> place,
>   it won't be a dead end—
> Because I am God, your personal God,
>   The Holy of Israel, your Savior.
> I paid a huge price for you:
> Isaiah 43:1-2 (The Message)

Thought:

How many times have you heard someone mutter "worthless" under his or her breath? If you listen closely, sometimes you hear "I'm" before "worthless". Do you ever catch yourself saying something similar -"Loser", "Stupid", "Nobody"?

Stop it.

While it's tough to change that thinking on your own, you can renew your mind by the word of God. The Holy Spirit can quicken the thoughts of God for you. He can make them come alive and change you from the inside out.

Although there are many solid Christians reading this right now, I know we are all connected to people who need to live the truth of how God sees them. So I'm just going to point you to 40DaysFromNegativity. com. We have a tool to help everyone personalize his or her identity in Christ. Click on the logo on the top left-hand side, fill in your name – or the name of your kids – or the name of someone you are going to email to encourage. Press the button and print off your personalized Identity in Christ.

I did the following for my daughter Taiessa. This is just the first part, because today we need to know that in Christ, you are valuable.

Taya Is Valuable.

John 1:12 Taya is God's daughter.

But Taya received Him, and to Taya He gave the right to become God's daughter, because Taya believes in His name.

John 15:5 Taya is a part of the true vine, and a channel of Christ's life.

I am the vine. Taya is a branch. If Taya remains in Me, and I in her, she will bear much fruit, for apart from Me, Taya can do nothing.

John 15:15 Taya is a friend of Christ.

No longer do I call Taya a servant, for a servant doesn't know what her lord does. But I have called Taya a friend, for everything that I heard from My Father, I have made known to Taya.

Rom. 8:17 Taya is a joint heir with Christ,
she shares Christ's inheritance with Him.

And if a daughter, then an heir; an heir of God,
and a joint-heir with Christ; if indeed Taya suffers
with Him, that Taya may also be glorified with Him.

I Cor. 3:9 Taya is God's co-worker.

For Taya is one of God's fellow workers.
Taya is God's field, God's building.

I Cor. 3:16   Taya is God's temple.

Don't you know that Taya is a temple of
God, and that God's Spirit lives in her?

Eph. 1:5-6 Taya has been adopted
by God as His daughter.

Having predestined Taya for adoption as
a daughter through Jesus Christ to Himself,
according to the good pleasure of His desire, to
the praise of the glory of His grace, by which He
freely bestowed favor on Taya in the Beloved.

Eph. 1:11 Taya has an inheritance in Christ.

In Him also Taya was assigned an
inheritance, having been predestined
according to the purpose of Him who works
all things after the counsel of His will.

from 10 minutes a day

Eph. 2:5-6 Taya has been made alive with Christ and she is seated with Christ in the heavenly places.

Even when Taya was dead in her trespasses, God made her alive together with Christ (by grace Taya has been saved), and raised Taya up with Him and made Taya to sit with Him in the heavenly places in Christ Jesus.

Eph. 2:10 Taya is God's workmanship, His handiwork.

For Taya is His workmanship, created in Christ Jesus for good works, which God prepared before that Taya should walk in them.

Col. 1:27 Christ Himself is in Taya.

To whom God was pleased to make known what are the riches of the glory of this mystery among the Gentiles, which is Christ in Taya, the hope of glory.

Col. 3:3 Taya 's life is hidden with Christ in God.

For Taya died, and her life is hidden with Christ in God.

Taiessa is valuable because God places His value on her, and so are you, because He does the same for you.

Prayer:

*Lord, forgive me for repeating the words
of death spoken over my life. Thank You
for the words of life that flow from You.
Thank You for calling me valuable – for
calling me a child, a friend, an inheritor, a
co-worker, and Your workmanship. Thank
you, Lord, for not making any junk.*

Challenge:

Speak these words of life over yourself today. If you
have an accountability partner, speak them over him
or her as well. The words of life come from Christ.
We need to speak the same.

Declaration:

I choose to believe what God says about me.
I choose to live out of what I choose to believe.
I choose to replace the lies that have attached
themselves to wounds from my past with the truth of
how God sees my situation and me.

from 10 minutes a day

Day 20 -
I Am Loved

Truth:

> *O LORD, God of heaven, the great and*
> *awesome God, who keeps his covenant*
> *of love with those who love him and*
> *obey his commands, Nehemiah 1:5*
> *(New International Version)*

Thought:

Most people never see this in me because I'm socially bold, but I am really rather shy. I get my energy when I'm alone. I don't "need" people to be around. I'm an introvert... although when I say that, people who know me laugh.

But if you're the least bit introverted, you may find all the "one another" commands a little overwhelming... here are just a few:

> *Romans 12:10 (NIV)*
> *Be devoted to one another in brotherly*
> *love. Honor one another above*
> *yourselves.*

> *Romans 12:16 (NIV)*
> *Live in harmony with one another. Do*
> *not be proud, but be willing to associate*
> *with people of low position. Do not be*
> *conceited.*

LIFE ABOVE the Negativity

Romans 14:13 (NIV)
Therefore let us stop passing judgment
on one another. Instead, make up your
mind not to put any stumbling block or
obstacle in your brother's or sister's way.

Romans 15:7 (NIV)
Accept one another, then, just as Christ
accepted you, in order to bring praise to
God.

1 Corinthians 1:10 (NIV)
I appeal to you, in the name of our Lord
Jesus Christ, that all of you agree with one
another so that there may be no divisions
among you and that you may be perfectly
united in mind and thought.

Galatians 5:13 (NIV)
You, my brothers, were called to be free.
But do not use your freedom to indulge
the sinful nature; rather, serve one
another in love.

Ephesians 4:32 (NIV)
Be kind and compassionate to one
another, forgiving each other, just as in
Christ God forgave you.

Ephesians 4:2 (NIV)
Be completely humble and gentle; be
patient, bearing with one another in love.

Ephesians 5:21 (NIV)
Submit to one another out of reverence
for Christ.

from 10 minutes a day

LIFE ABOVE the Negativity

Colossians 3:13 (NIV)
Bear with each other and forgive
whatever grievances you may have
against one another. Forgive as the Lord
forgave you.

1 Thessalonians 5:11 (NIV)
Therefore encourage one another and
build each other up, just as in fact you
are doing.

Hebrews 3:13 (NIV)
But encourage one another daily, as long
as it is called Today, so that none of you
may be hardened by sin's deceitfulness.

Hebrews 10:24 (NIV)
And let us consider how we may spur
one another on toward love and good
deeds.

Hebrews 10:25 (NIV)
Let us not give up meeting together, as
some are in the habit of doing, but let us
encourage one another—and all the more
as you see the Day approaching.

1 Peter 1:22 (NIV)
Now that you have purified yourselves by
obeying the truth so that you have sincere
love for your brothers, love one another
deeply, from the heart.

1 Peter 3:8 (NIV)
Finally, all of you, live in harmony with
one another; be sympathetic, love as
brothers, be compassionate and humble.

1 Peter 5:5 (NIV)
Young men, in the same way be
submissive to those who are older. All
of you, clothe yourselves with humility
toward one another, because, "God
opposes the proud but gives grace to the
humble."

I could be intimidated by that list too, but I've learned a secret so that it's not difficult for me to fulfill these commands. I've found that when I'm a friend with someone, I naturally do all of these things.

I have patience for them, I rejoice with them, I cry with them, I encourage them, I forgive them, I give way to them, I honor them and I look out for their interests. My secret is to make friends.

And I make friends knowing I can show them love, because God has shown love to me.

1 John 4:11 (NIV)
Dear friends, since God so loved us, we
also ought to love one another.

Because God loves us, we can show love that's sincere to others.

Aren't you convinced that you're loved? If you've printed off your personalized Identity in Christ then read it to yourself and study the verses until you're convinced. If you haven't printed it off, go to 40DaysFromNegativity.com and do it right now.

Paul prayed for you when he prayed for the church in Ephesus:

> *And I pray that you, being rooted and*
> *established in love, may have power,*
> *together with all the saints, to grasp*
> *how wide and long and high and deep*
> *is the love of Christ, and to know this*
> *love that surpasses knowledge—that you*
> *may be filled to the measure of all the*
> *fullness of God. Ephesians 3:17-19 (New*
> *International Version)*

If you don't believe it, make sure to print off the personalized book of Ephesians when you're at the site.

You are loved! Be filled with God's love!

Prayer:

> *Oh Lord, that I would know the width and*
> *height and depth of Your love for me, so that*
> *I may experience this love that surpasses*
> *understanding. Lord, let Your love surround and*
> *encompass me so that it overflows from me to*
> *all You've placed in my web of relationships.*

Challenge:

Do you feel like a really big challenge today? Memorize your personalized Identity in Christ. Repeat the "I am Loved" portion out loud until you can say it in your sleep.

Declaration:

I choose to believe what God says about me. I choose to live out of what I choose to believe. I choose to replace the lies that have attached themselves to wounds from my past with the truth of how God sees my situation and me.

from 10 minutes a day

LIFE ABOVE the Negativity

Day 21 -
I Am Victorious

Truth:

> *Can anything ever separate us from Christ's love? Does it mean he no longer loves us if we have trouble or calamity, or are persecuted, or hungry, or destitute, or in danger, or threatened with death? As the Scriptures say, "For your sake we are killed every day; we are being slaughtered like sheep." No, despite all these things, overwhelming victory is ours through Christ, who loved us. Romans 8:35-37 (New Living Translation)*

Thought:

Why is a clock that is five minutes late more dangerous than one that is five hours early?

Because we pick up on lies that are way off, but the ones that seem to be truth we can more easily trust.

What did satan do when he tempted Christ in the desert? He used the truth about Jesus' situation and the partial truth from the word of God to tempt Christ into believing his version of the truth.

And he uses the same tactic with us today.

How often do we live as if we believe "the overwhelming victory is ours through Christ?" Be honest. It's usually the trouble or calamity, or persecution, or hunger, or destitution, or danger, or threats of death that really grab our attention.

from 10 minutes a day

It's time we replace those lies with the truth. I've used my son Kian as an example, but if you haven't done it yet, go to 40DaysFromNegativity.com and print off your own personalized Identity in Christ. It is so critical we live out of how God sees us. This is simply a tool to get it into your thinking.

Kian Is Victorious.

John 8:31-32 Kian has been set free.

If Kian remains in My word, then he is truly My disciple. Kian will know the truth, and the truth will make him free.

Rom. 6:1-4 Kian died with Christ and he died to the power of sin's rule over his life.

What shall we say then? Shall Kian continue in sin, that grace may abound? May it never be! If Kian died to sin, how could he live in it any longer? Or don't you know that when Kian was baptized into Christ Jesus, he was baptized into His death? Kian was buried with Him through baptism to death, that just as Christ was raised from the dead through the glory of the Father, so Kian also might walk in newness of life.

Rom. 8:37 Kian is more than a conqueror in Christ.

No, in all these things, Kian is more than a conqueror through Him who loved him.

II Cor. 2:14 Kian is led triumphantly by Christ.

But thanks be to God, who always leads Kian in triumph in Christ, and reveals through Kian the sweet aroma of His knowledge in every place.

Gal. 2:20 Kian was crucified with Christ.

Kian has been crucified with Christ, and it is no longer Kian who lives, but Christ living in him. That life which Kian now lives in the flesh, he lives by faith in the Son of God, who loved Kian, and gave Himself up for him.

Phil. 4:13 Kian can do all things through Christ.

Kian can do all things through Christ, who strengthens him.

II Tim. 1:7 Kian has been given a spirit of power, love and self-discipline.

For God didn't give Kian a spirit of fear, but of power and love and self-discipline.

I John 5:4-5 Kian has overcome the world.

For Kian is born of God and overcomes the world. This is the victory that has overcome the world: Kian's faith. Kian overcomes the world because he believes that Jesus is the Son of God.

What is true with Kian is true for you. When your circumstance – even though it can be through no fault of your own - is contrary to the will of God expressed in Scripture, are you going to believe the Bible or your circumstance?

Having Jesus as your Lord means He's in the driver's seat of your life. It means when my life doesn't line up with Scripture, I change my life to agree with God. I can't ignore truth that He's revealed and I can't say it doesn't apply to me.

You are victorious. Believe it and live it!

Prayer:

Lord, forgive me for looking at my circumstance instead of trusting in Your truth. When life in a fallen world happens, I haven't always run to You as I should have. I know Your plans for me are good because You are good. I know Your plans are to prosper me and not to harm me and to give me a hope and a future. I know that in Christ I am more than a conqueror and I choose to praise You in the storm.

Challenge:

Take the verses listed under the "Kian is Victorious" section, look them up and meditate on them. Think about how much God loves you, despite your circumstance and praise Him before the answer comes.

Declaration:

I choose to believe what God says about me. I choose to live out of what I choose to believe. I choose to replace the lies that have attached themselves to wounds from my past with the truth of how God sees my situation and me.

Day 22 -
I am Chosen

Truth:

> *Even before he made the world, God*
> *loved us and chose us in Christ to be holy*
> *and without fault in his eyes. Ephesians*
> *1:4 (New Living Translation)*

Thought:

"I am not my own. I have been bought with a price. I belong to God. I have been chosen before the foundation of the world. I have been set apart and called holy. I am His." These are words I often find coming from my lips to remind myself and satan whose I am. They just bubble up to encourage me.

I have had the experience of hearing the audible voice of God set me apart and it absolutely wrecked my life. I can only explain it as feeling so insignificant and yet so highly valued that the only response left to me was unadulterated awe.

Sixteen years later, I know it wasn't just for a moment in time. We are receiving a kingdom that cannot be shaken so we need to worship Him acceptably with all reverence and awe, because our God is a consuming fire (Hebrews 12:28-29).

So why do we relate to Him only as a friend?

Being chosen by a friend, really isn't that significant. Being chosen by the one who spoke the 400 million stars in this galaxy and the 400 million galaxies in this universe and potentially unlimited universes into

Life ABOVE the Negativity

being is highly significant.

It is for me… and it needs to be for you.

You are chosen, set apart, taught, loved and empowered by the Great I AM, the ever-living Father, the Alpha and Omega, the First and the Last - GOD.

How life-wrecking is that?

Oh, that you may have the spirit of wisdom and revelation that you may know the hope to which you have been called, the glorious inheritance in the saints and the incomparably great power for all who believe.

A friend sent this to me in an email. I usually don't pass them along, but this one caught my eye. Why do you think it's shaped like a bell? I think it's because we all need a wake up call to our true identity in Christ.

I've had to include it on the next page...

LIFE ABOVE the Negativity

I KNOW WHO I AM

I am God's child (John 1:12)

I am Christ's friend (John 15:15)

I am united with the Lord(1 Cor. 6:17)

I am bought with a price(1 Cor. 6:19-20)

I am a saint (set apart for God). (Eph. 1:1)

I am a personal witness of Christ (Acts 1:8)

I am the salt & light of the earth (Matt.5:13-14)

I am a member of the body of Christ(1 Cor 12:27)

I am free forever from condemnation (Rom. 8: 1-2)

I am a citizen of Heaven. I am significant (Phil.3:20)

I am free from any charge against me (Rom. 8:31-34)

I am a minister of reconciliation for God(2 Cor.5:17-21)

I have access to God through the Holy Spirit (Eph. 2:18)

I am seated with Christ in the heavenly realms (Eph. 2:6)

I cannot be separated from the love of God(Rom.8:35-39)

I am established, anointed, sealed by God (2 Cor.1:21-22)

I am assured all things work together for good (Rom. 8: 28)

I have been chosen and appointed to bear fruit (John 15:16)

I may approach God with freedom and confidence (Eph. 3: 12)

I can do all things through Christ who strengthens me (Phil. 4:13)

I am the branch of the true vine, a channel of His life (John 15: 1-5)

I am God's temple (1 Cor. 3: 16). I am complete in Christ (Col. 2: 10)

I am hidden with Christ in God (Col. 3:3).
I have been justified (Romans 5:1)

I am God's co-worker (1 Cor. 3:9; 2 Cor 6:1).
I am God's workmanship(Eph. 2:10)

I am confident that the good works God has
begun in me will be perfected (Phil. 1: 5)

I have been redeemed and forgiven (Col. 1:14). I
have been adopted as God's child(Eph 1:5)

I belong to God

Do you know

who you are!?

You're chosen. The accuser can't touch you. Know who you are in Christ and live out of that revelation today.

Prayer:

> *Eternal Father, grant me the spirit of wisdom and revelation so that I will know the hope to which I have been called, the glorious inheritance in the saints and the incomparably great power for all who believe. I am Yours. I have been bought with a price. I belong to You. I have been chosen before the foundation of the world.*

Challenge:

Go over all the truths in the personalized Identity in Christ you printed off from 40DaysFromNegativity. com. We didn't have time to cover them all directly, but other the next few days we'll be covering some of them from another angle. They are truth and truth is life so read them, pray them, declare them, pronounce them, know them, and live out of them.

Declaration:

I choose to believe what God says about me. I choose to live out of what I choose to believe. I choose to replace the lies that have attached themselves to wounds from my past with the truth of how God sees my situation and me.

from 10 minutes a day

Day 23 -
<u>God Has Forgiven Me</u>

Truth:

> *If we say we have no sin [refusing to admit that we are sinners], we delude and lead ourselves astray, and the Truth [which the Gospel presents] is not in us [does not dwell in our hearts]. If we [freely] admit that we have sinned and confess our sins, He is faithful and just (true to His own nature and promises) and will forgive our sins [dismiss our lawlessness] and [continuously] cleanse us from all unrighteousness [everything not in conformity to His will in purpose, thought, and action]. If we say (claim) we have not sinned, we contradict His Word and make Him out to be false and a liar, and His Word is not in us [the divine message of the Gospel is not in our hearts]. 1 John 1:8-10 (Amplified Bible)*

Thought:

Are you a follower of Christ who struggles with having a victorious daily walk with the Lord?

If so, it may be because of the sin of un-forgiveness. God cannot violate his perfect nature and overlook our sin. Un-forgiveness is a common stronghold the devil has in the lives of many of God's children. We believe lies about forgiveness and live according to those lies.

You do not need to be perfect before Christ forgives

you and welcomes you into His kingdom. He loves you the way you are… and wants to empower you to forgive others, to be forgiven by others, and to accept the forgiveness He freely offers you.

You can arrive at this by first admitting you've fallen short of the impossible standard of a Perfect God… you're not perfect.

We're all ready to admit that, but most of us use it as an excuse not to do better and don't understand what that means to the reality of life.

When we say, "I'm only human," it's only true in the sense that we're only fallen humans. We are not what we were created to be.

> *When Adam sinned, sin entered the entire human race. Adam's sin brought death, so death spread to everyone, for everyone sinned.*
> *Romans 5:12 NLT*

We were created to be in close relationship with our Creator. We were created to not be separated from God, His creation, our partners, and ourselves and yet this is our reality.

Since sin came into the world, we have been separated from our true identities. We are separated from others and separated from creation. Perhaps most importantly, we are separated from the one who created us and saw every one of our days before one of them came to be.

But that changes when you admit you've fallen short… admit that you've sinned. The Bible says when we confess our sins; God will forgive us and cleanse us.

> *If we claim to be without sin, we deceive ourselves and the truth is not in us. If we confess our sins, he is faithful and just and will forgive us our sins and purify us from all unrighteousness. If we claim we have not sinned, we make him out to be a liar and his word has no place in our lives.*
> *1 John 1:8-10 (NIV)*

This is what happens when you tell God you're sorry and decide to live your life with the knowledge that Jesus is in the driver's seat of your life.

When your life doesn't line up with Scripture, you change your life so that it does. You don't ignore what the Bible says or complain, "It's too difficult." If God wants you to do something, He'll empower you to do it.

Now some of you are saying "I already knew all that." Great. Maybe you need to share it with someone else today?

But I want you to ask yourself, "Have I worked out its implication into every area of my life?"

If you have started, then God can empower you to do the difficult things we are going to discuss over the next few days. They are part of His will, so He'll help you to do them.

Prayer:

> *Lord, Thank you for Your forgiveness. Thank You that as I confess my sins to You, You are faithful and just to forgive me my sins and to cleanse me from all unrighteousness. Thank You, Holy Spirit, that You empower me to do the will of God. Thank You for preparing me for a deeper walk with You.*

Challenge:

Thank God for forgiving you of your confessed sins. Thank Him for forgiving the ones you remember. Thank Him for forgiving the ones that you've since forgot. Ask God if you need to forgive someone else.

Declaration:

I choose to forgive everyone who has wronged me. I choose to seek the forgiveness of those I have wronged. I choose to accept I have been forgiven of my confessed sin. I choose to walk in the freedom forgiveness brings.

from 10 minutes a day

Day 24 -
<u>Forgiveness Confusion</u>

Truth:

> *Bear with each other and forgive*
> *whatever grievances you may have*
> *against one another. Forgive as the Lord*
> *forgave you. (Colossians 3:13 NIV)*

Thought:

Too many followers of Christ are confused about forgiveness. They live out of lies they hold to as truth. We'll be looking at some of those lies today.

We don't forgive because we believe the violator needs to pay. We feel the one who did us wrong needs to understand what we were put through. We want the one who sinned to acknowledge what they did and make amends.

But we must awaken to the fact that un-forgiveness leads to bitterness and separation from God. He has forgiven us and wants to enable us to make the choice to forgive those who have sinned against us.

Here are some questions I've come across over the years. If someone else has asked them, I know other people are thinking them. Let's use Scripture to clear up the confusion.

Q. Does the offender pay if I don't forgive?

A. No. But you pay. You only harm yourself when you refuse to forgive wrongs done to you.

Life ABOVE the Negativity

For if you forgive others their trespasses, your heavenly Father will also forgive you; but if you do not forgive others, neither will your Father forgive your trespasses.(Matthew 6:14-15 NRSV)

If you forgive others, you will be forgiven.
(Luke 6:37 NLT)

Un-forgiveness is a sin God cannot look upon. It separates us from our loving Creator. If you want to see how serious it is, check out Jesus' parable of the unrepentant servant in Matthew 18:21-35.

Q. Does forgiving someone let him or her "off the hook"?

A. No. It puts them into God's hands.

Do not take revenge, my friends, but leave room for God's wrath, for it is written: "It is mine to avenge; I will repay," says the Lord. (Romans 12:19 NIV)

Q. Shouldn't I wait until they change before I forgive?

A. No.

Forgive as Christ forgave you (Col 3:13).

How is that?

While we were still sinners, Christ died for us. (Rom 5:8).

Before we deserved it… He showed us grace. You must choose to forgive whoever has wronged you. We forgive for the sake of our relationship with God, not for the sake of the other person.

Q.But Christ doesn't forgive me until I ask for it, so shouldn't I wait to forgive someone until they ask for it?

A. No. First, you aren't God. You don't have His capacity for grace. Second, understand that you forgive for your sake, not theirs. Christ said in Matthew 18 that if we don't forgive another from our hearts, tormentors will be assigned to us. If you don't forgive someone until they ask for forgiveness, you're actually letting them keep you imprisoned.

Q. Shouldn't I wait until I feel like forgiving?

A. Don't wait until you feel like forgiving… you never will. Forgiveness is a choice, a decision of your will.

> Make allowance for each other's faults,
> and forgive anyone who offends you.
> Remember, the Lord forgave you, so
> you must forgive others. Colossians 3:13
> (New Living Translation)

Q. Do I need to trust someone I forgive?

A. No. Forgiveness and trust are two separate issues.

Forgiveness is given while trust is earned. Forgiving someone does not mean they don't face the consequences for their actions. It does not mean you put yourself into harm's way. You are not a doormat for those who would hurt you.

Now you may have other misconceptions about forgiveness, and we may cover some in the next couple of days. But many followers of Christ stumble on these points. So even if you're not struggling with forgiving someone, you are close to someone who is. Help them to find the freedom of forgiveness.

Prayer:

In the name of Jesus, I purpose and choose to forgive (the person) from my heart for (what they did). I acknowledge the hurt and the hate it has led to in my life and I agree to live with the consequences of their sin.

In the name of Jesus I cancel all the debts and obligations to me. I release (the person) to You, as well as my right to avenge.

Dear Lord, I ask You to forgive me for my bitterness toward (the person) in this situation. In the name of Jesus and in the power of His blood, I cancel satan's power over me in this memory because I have forgiven and have been forgiven by God.

In the name of Jesus, I command that all the tormentors that have been assigned to me because of my un-forgiveness leave me now.

Holy Spirit, I invite You into my heart and to heal me from this pain. Please speak Your words of truth to me about this situation.

This I pray in the name of Jesus Christ my Lord. Amen

LIFE ABOVE the Negativity

Challenge:

Ask God to reveal to you anyone that you may need to forgive. As you wait on Him, you may be surprised at who He brings to your mind. Choose to forgive them and release them into God's hands.

Declaration:

I choose to forgive everyone who has wronged me. I choose to seek the forgiveness of those I have wronged. I choose to accept I have been forgiven of my confessed sin. I choose to walk in the freedom forgiveness brings.

Day 25 - When You Remember the Pain

Truth:

> *I have thought deeply about all that goes on here under the sun, where people have the power to hurt each other. I have seen wicked people buried with honor. Yet they were the very ones who frequented the Temple and are now praised in the same city where they committed their crimes! This, too, is meaningless. When a crime is not punished quickly, people feel it is safe to do wrong. But even though a person sins a hundred times and still lives a long time, I know that those who fear God will be better off. Ecclesiastes 8:9-12 (New Living Translation)*

Thought:

Another lie we believe about forgiveness is that "If I can't forget, than I haven't forgiven." Don't you love it when people quote adages like they're Scripture? "Forgive and forget" has done so much damage to people's understanding of God and their relationship with others.

Do you realize God does not forget the sins He forgives us of? How could He and still be an all-knowing God? Instead He chooses to not remember and hold them against us.

from 10 minutes a day

"For I will forgive their wickedness and will remember their sins no more."
(Jeremiah 31:34 NIV)

Then he adds: "Their sins and lawless acts I will remember no more." (Hebrews 10:17 NIV)

This is more than just an exercise in semantics. We also can't easily forget. God has created us with minds to remember. Thoughts will pop back into our minds and we have no power over the past...but we do have control over how we let our past control our present and our future.

When memories come, of hurts and pains you have chosen to forgive, don't try to ignore them. Remember the whole event - including the FACT you have chosen to forgive them with the strength God provides.

Dr. Chuck Lynch in his book "I Should Forgive, But..." gives this advice regarding the obsessive thinking that often surrounds forgiven hurts:

1. **Address God** - Stating God's name in a firm way forcibly stops the obsessive thinking, but usually only momentarily. It is the starting point at dealing with dangerous thoughts.

2. **Thank God** - Express appreciation to God for allowing you to remember the past offense you had to forgive. This allows you to review this biblical tool which Christ illustrated at the time of His own hurt and rejection "Father,

from 10 minutes a day

forgive them…" It will also bring to mind that you have left them with God. You can thank Him that you were able to give the same gift of forgiveness you received and thus reflect God's character to others.

3. **Praise God** - Sincerely praise God for the tool of forgiveness. Praise Him for forgiving you as you forgive others and for what He's going to do through this experience for His glory.

Over time, we can forget many of the worse things done to us. But we don't get to that place by trying to forget.

The secret is to remember the whole truth, including the fact you've chosen to forgive. This is how you release yourself from the lie of the enemy that says you need to forget if you truly forgive.

Choose to remember the whole truth today.

Prayer:

Lord, thank You I am fearfully and wonderfully made. Thank You for creating me with a mind to remember. The enemy has wanted to use that for evil, but I choose to remember the good things of You, including the fact You empowered me to forgive.

LIFE ABOVE the Negativity

Challenge:

If this truth was for you today, then apply it to your life. If remembering pain isn't your problem right now, be a light in a dark world and share this truth with someone who needs it today. Walk with them as they journey through the pain.

Declaration:

I choose to forgive everyone who has wronged me. I choose to seek the forgiveness of those I have wronged. I choose to accept I have been forgiven of my confessed sin. I choose to walk in the freedom forgiveness brings.

Day 26 -
When You
Need Forgiveness

Truth:

> ...leave your sacrifice there at the altar.
> Go and be reconciled to that person.
> Then come and offer your sacrifice
> to God. Matthew 5:24 (New Living
> Translation)

Thought:

We are fallen people living in a fallen world. That's not an excuse. We need to become more and more and more like Jesus. But there may be times when we have sinned against someone else and we need to make it right.

The rabbis taught that the sin against someone else was heavier than the sin against God, because God would always forgive, but someone else may not.

They didn't have the book of Romans, so Rabbi Paul had a different point of view we follow, but more about that in a bit. Jesus gave us a pattern to follow in Matthew 5:23-26

> "So if you are presenting a sacrifice at
> the altar in the Temple and you suddenly
> remember that someone has something
> against you, leave your sacrifice there

from 10 minutes a day

*at the altar. Go and be reconciled to
that person. Then come and offer your
sacrifice to God. When you are on the
way to court with your adversary, settle
your differences quickly. Otherwise, your
accuser may hand you over to the judge,
who will hand you over to an officer, and
you will be thrown into prison. And if that
happens, you surely won't be free again
until you have paid the last penny. (New
Living Translation)*

There are a couple of things I'll point out right away.
It's the one bringing the sacrifice that remembers
someone has something against him or her. It's the
Holy Spirit that brings it to their mind. It's the Spirit's
job to convict sin, not any of ours. Jesus Christ didn't
come into the world to condemn it, so how can we
condemn a fellow believer (or the world for that
matter)?

Neil T. Anderson gives the following advice in *"The
Steps to Freedom in Christ"*:

Only the actions, which have hurt another
person, need to be confessed to them. If you
have had jealous, lustful or angry thoughts
toward another, and they don't know about
it, these are to be confessed to God alone.
An exception to this principle occurs when
restitution needs to be made. If you stole
or broke something, damaged someone's
reputation, and so on, you need to go to that
person and make it right, even if he or she is
unaware of what you did.

The Process of Seeking Forgiveness

1. Write out what you did wrong and why you did it.

2. Make sure you have already forgiven the person for whatever he or she may have done to you.

3. Think through exactly how you will ask him or her to forgive you. Be sure to

a. Label your action as wrong.

b. Be specific and admit what you did.

c. Make no defenses or excuses.

d. Do not blame the other person, and do not expect or demand that he or she ask for your forgiveness.

e. Your confession should lead to the direct question: "Will you forgive me?"

4. Seek the right place and the right time to approach the offended person.

5. Ask for forgiveness in person from anyone with whom you can talk face-to-face with the following exception: Do not go alone when your safety might be in danger.

from 10 minutes a day

6. Except where no other means of communication is possible, do not write a letter because a letter can be very easily misread or misunderstood; a letter can be read by the wrong people (those having nothing to do with the offense or the confession); a letter can be kept when it should have been destroyed.

Now remember what I said about Rabbi Paul? Here's where his teaching comes in. Once you sincerely seek forgiveness, you are free-whether the other person forgives you or not. Paul wrote in Romans 12:18:

> Do all that you can to live in peace with everyone.
> (New Living Translation)

So once you've sincerely sought forgiveness, you are free. So be sure to do what Jesus said in Matthew 5:24:

> ...leave your sacrifice there at the altar.
> Go and be reconciled to that person.
> Then come and offer your sacrifice to
> God. (New Living Translation)

Asking forgiveness from someone we've wronged can be a very difficult thing to do. But now that you know the truth, remember the whole truth – God has not only told you to do it, He'll empower you to do it. It may be good to discuss these thoughts with your pastor if you need some support in doing what the

Bible instructs you.

We're praying for you.

Prayer:

> *Lord, thank You once again for forgiving me of all my sins. Thank You for cleansing me and making me a minister of reconciliation. If I have sinned against someone I need to ask forgiveness from, bring him or her to my memory and make it possible for me to seek reconciliation. Holy Spirit, help me do what pleases the Father.*

Challenge:

Is there someone you need to ask forgiveness from? Ask the Holy Spirit to remind you of anyone you may not be in right relationship with. Wait in His presence and expect Him to speak. When images or thoughts go through your mind, confess them to God if you need to, and seek the forgiveness of others if you must.

Declaration:

I choose to forgive everyone who has wronged me. I choose to seek the forgiveness of those I have wronged. I choose to accept I have been forgiven of my confessed sin. I choose to walk in the freedom forgiveness brings.

from 10 minutes a day

Day 27 -
How to Accept That
<u>You Have Been Forgiven</u>

Truth:

> *Jesus said to the people who believed in him, "You are truly my disciples if you remain faithful to my teachings. And you will know the truth, and the truth will set you free." John 8:31-33 (New Living Translation)*

Thought:

There are many who, after being forgiven by God and after seeking the forgiveness of those they have offended, find it extremely difficult to live in the freedom that forgiveness brings.

Sometimes they don't feel they were worthy to be forgiven. This is true; all of us stand before God by His grace. But this is a liberating truth of scripture, not something that condemns us.

> *Therefore, there is now no condemnation for those who are in Christ Jesus, (Romans 8:1 NIV)*

The best thing you can do to accept that you have been forgiven is to build your faith in this area by knowing what the Bible says regarding the forgiveness of confessed sins. Because:

*...faith [comes] by hearing, and hearing
by the word of God.
(Romans 10:17 NKJV)*

The following verses assure us that we are forgiven when we confess our sins. Remember - believe what the Bible says about you... not what your feelings say!

Read them.

Memorize them.

Meditate on them.

Let them become alive to you. It's the living word of God that makes faith come alive. Pray them whenever you feel the condemning attack of satan saying you're not forgiven.

*If we claim to be without sin, we deceive
ourselves and the truth is not in us. If we
confess our sins, he is faithful and just
and will forgive us our sins and purify us
from all unrighteousness.
(1 John 1:8-9 NIV)*

*Cleanse me with hyssop, and I will be
clean; wash me, and I will be whiter than
snow.
(Psalms 51:7 NIV)*

*...who forgives all your sins and heals
all your diseases, who redeems your life
from the pit and crowns you with love
and compassion,
(Psalms 103:3-4 NIV)*

*"Come now, let us reason together," says
the LORD. "Though your sins are like
scarlet, they shall be as white as snow;
though they are red as crimson, they shall
be like wool.
(Isaiah 1:18 NIV)*

*Peter replied, "Repent and be baptized,
every one of you, in the name of Jesus
Christ for the forgiveness of your sins.
And you will receive the gift of the Holy
Spirit.
(Acts 2:38 NIV)*

*Are any among you suffering? They
should keep on praying about it. And
those who have reason to be thankful
should continually sing praises to the
Lord. Are any among you sick? They
should call for the elders of the church
and have them pray over them, anointing
them with oil in the name of the Lord.
And their prayer offered in faith will heal
the sick, and the Lord will make them
well. And anyone who has committed
sins will be forgiven. Confess your sins
to each other and pray for each other
so that you may be healed. The earnest
prayer of a righteous person has great
power and wonderful results.*

(James 5:13-16 NLT)

*My dear children, I write this to you
so that you will not sin. But if anybody
does sin, we have one who speaks to the
Father in our defense— Jesus Christ, the
Righteous One. He is the atoning sacrifice
for our sins, and not only for ours but also
for the sins of the whole world.*
(1 John 2:1-2 NIV)

*People who cover over their sins will
not prosper. But if they confess and
forsake them, they will receive mercy.*
(Proverbs 28:13 NLT)

You are forgiven from sin that you confess. Work these verses into your thinking if you need to, and pass the truth along to others you can encourage.

Prayer:

*Lord, show me Your love for me. Reveal
Your passion once more. Thank You for Your
forgiveness. Thank You for Your grace. Thank
You for Your mercy. Thank You for Your strength.
Release Your people to walk in the knowledge
they are forgiven and they are Yours.*

from 10 minutes a day

Challenge:

Memorize these verses and meditate on them. If they aren't for you right now, they will be for someone God brings along your path. Share the truth of God's love for them.

Declaration:

I choose to forgive everyone who has wronged me. I choose to seek the forgiveness of those I have wronged. I choose to accept I have been forgiven of my confessed sin. I choose to walk in the freedom forgiveness brings.

Day 28 -
Agreeing to Live Without
<u>What God Withholds</u>

Truth:

Oh, that you would rend the heavens and come down,
>*that the mountains would tremble before you!*
As when fire sets twigs ablaze
>*and causes water to boil,*
>*come down to make your name known to your enemies and cause the nations to quake before you!*
For when you did awesome things that we did not expect, you came down, and the mountains trembled before you.
Since ancient times no one has heard,
>*no ear has perceived,*
>*no eye has seen any God besides you,*
>*who acts on behalf of those who wait for him.*
You come to the help of those who gladly do right,
>*who remember your ways.*
>*But when we continued to sin against them,*
>*you were angry.*
>*How then can we be saved?*
All of us have become like one who is unclean,
>*and all our righteous acts are like filthy rags;*

> we all shrivel up like a leaf,
>> and like the wind our sins sweep us
> away.
>> No one calls on your name
>>> or strives to lay hold of you;
>>>> for you have hidden your face from
> us
>>> and made us waste away because of
> our sins.
>> Yet, O LORD, you are our Father.
>>> We are the clay, you are the potter;
>>> we are all the work of your hand.
> *Isaiah 64:1-8 (New International Version)*

Thought:

I've often been asked if anyone ever needs to forgive God. That language makes me uncomfortable.

Forgiveness is giving up our right for revenge. It's putting the other into the hands of God. It's His to avenge. He's the one to repay. How can we put God in His own hands? How could we ever take revenge against God?

However, forgiveness is also agreeing to live with the consequences of another's action or inaction. That could mean we may need to forgive God... but the language and sentiment isn't right.

I'm in debt to Bill Johnson for giving me biblical words to express how we need to relate to God when things happen that just don't make sense in light of His nature or character.

It comes from what John the Baptist had his disciples ask Jesus, while John sat in prison awaiting his fate.

John the Baptist declared the Lamb of God who takes away the sin of the world, knowing the Anointed One would release the prisoners. But then he sat in prison and doubt started to set in. He sent his disciples to ask his cousin if he had gotten it wrong and Jesus responded:

> *"Go and tell John the things you have seen and heard: that the blind see, the lame walk, the lepers are cleansed, the deaf hear, the dead are raised, the poor have the gospel preached to them. And blessed is he who is not offended because of Me." Luke 7:22-23 (NKJV)*

John was sitting where he did not expect, facing something he did not want. We could almost say he had the right to be offended at Jesus.

And Jesus said "happy is the one who is not offended because of Me."

We don't need to forgive God. We need to live un-offended with Him. Part of living un-offended at God is agreeing to live without what He withholds.

Are you in the place where your situation, through no fault of your own, is not in agreement with how the Bible says it should be?

For example, the Bible says in 1 Peter 2:24, "By His wounds we were healed." What happens when you're not?

Agreeing to live without what God withholds

means we don't create theology from our experience. We can't say, "It's not God's will for me to be healed." Because we know His will is done perfectly in heaven and we know in heaven there is no sickness so we know it's not His will for anyone to be sick. We cannot create theology from our experience.

Agreeing to live without what God withholds means we don't make excuses for God not to be true to His word. 'Oh, in heaven I'll be healed." So does that mean in heaven you'll finally be forgiven? David said in Psalm 103, "[the Lord] forgives all your sins and heals all your diseases." Why can we believe for one and not the other in this life? Don't make excuses for God.

Agreeing to live without what God withholds does not mean we can't change God's mind. "God will heal me in His time." I know this is controversial. But look at Abraham, and Moses, and Ezekiel and Mary and how they changed God's mind. The timing of God is real, but just as real is the fact that friends of God can change His mind. The timing of God is a convenient excuse we have made a theology out of.

Agreeing to live without what God withholds means letting the potter be the potter and recognize you are the clay. His ways are not our ways. His thoughts are not our thoughts. He thinks generationally and eternally. We are short sighted and linear. It's best for us to simply be still and know that He is God. (Psalm 46:10)

So be still, and know that He is God.

Prayer:

*Lord, that You would rend the heavens
and come down to make Your name known
and set all things right. I know You are
Good and I know You are Great. And I trust
You, God, to turn all things for the good of
those who love You and have been called
according to Your purpose. I choose to
live without what You choose to withhold,
knowing You are good and You are great.*

Challenge:

Instead of waiting for your situation to change, wait expectantly on God. Choose to still yourself by focusing on His love and goodness.

Declaration:

I choose to live un-offended at God. I agree with the Bible that God is Good and God is Great. Even though I don't understand my circumstance, I give up my right to understand so that I can have the peace that passes understanding.

LIFE ABOVE the Negativity

Day 29 - Look to What God is Doing, Not to What He Hasn't Done

Truth:

> "But forget all that—
>   it is nothing compared to what I am
> going to do.
> For I am about to do something new.
>   See, I have already begun! Do you
> not see it?
>   I will make a pathway through the
> wilderness.
>   I will create rivers in the dry
> wasteland."
> Isaiah 43:18-19 (New Living Translation)

Thought:

As we choose to live un-offended at God, we need to make a choice as to what we will focus on. Will our focus be on what He is doing or will it be on what hasn't been done?

This isn't simply a case of being an optimist, a pessimist or a realist. It's a spiritual choice we make to fix our thoughts on what is true, and honorable, and right, and pure, and lovely and admirable. And to think about things that are excellent and worthy of praise. Philippians 4:8 (New Living Translation)

We can't do that when all we see is what God hasn't done.

A tool to help us focus on the positive is testimony. Testimony is telling the truth about God to others. It is talking about His goodness and sharing about His greatness. It is reminding ourselves of the good things He's given us and done for us.

Look how powerful testimony is. In Revelation 12:11 it talks about the saints overcoming satan:

> They overcame him
> by the blood of the Lamb
> and by the word of their testimony;
> they did not love their lives so much
> as to shrink from death.
> Revelation 12:11 (New International Version)

Testimony is supernatural. Further on in Revelations chapter 19 verse ten it says:

> ..the testimony of Jesus is the spirit of prophecy. Revelation 19:10

Remind yourself about the good things of God. Tell others about the good things of God. Fix your thoughts on what is true, and honorable, and right, and pure, and lovely and admirable. And to think about things that are excellent and worthy of praise.

Focus on what God is doing and what He has done. Don't be fixated on what He hasn't done.

Did you know someone else's testimony could open the door for us to be offended at God? It easily can if our hearts aren't right.

Bill Johnson gives an example of a group of

from 10 minutes a day

Christians who were taken away, lined up and shot. The firing squad left and the ones on the ground got up and found holes in the shirts where the bullets entered and exited, but they had no wounds.

Incredible, right? Praise God. Amen. Send around the offering plate.

How about if your loved one was in another group of Christians who were shot and they didn't avoid being killed? How easy would it be to ask God – why them and not my loved one? How easy would it be for a testimony to be twisted by the enemy into a weapon that opens a fresh wound?

The condition of our heart is so critical. The focus of our eyes is so essential.

Focus on what God has done and what He is doing. Take what He hasn't done to Him in prayer. He's there to comfort, but I've learned He really doesn't seem to respond well to whining.

Prayer:

Lord forgive me for focusing on things You haven't done for me, instead of remembering every good and perfect gift that has come from You. Holy Spirit, help me to testify the God things of God. I agree with the word that says, "I am still confident of this, I will see the goodness of the Lord in the land of the living. I'll be strong and take heart and wait for the Lord."

from 10 minutes a day

Challenge:

Once again, instead of waiting for your situation to change, why not wait on God? Wait with expectation, knowing He is the giver of good gifts. Wait being ready to respond to the love He shows you.

Declaration:

I choose to live un-offended at God. I agree with the Bible that God is Good and God is Great. Even though I don't understand my circumstance, I give up my right to understand so that I can have the peace that passes understanding.

LIFE ABOVE the Negativity

Day 30 -
Give Up Your Right
to Understand

Truth:

> *Always be full of joy in the Lord. I say it again—rejoice! Let everyone see that you are considerate in all you do. Remember, the Lord is coming soon. Don't worry about anything; instead, pray about everything. Tell God what you need, and thank him for all he has done. Then you will experience God's peace, which exceeds anything we can understand. His peace will guard your hearts and minds as you live in Christ Jesus. Philippians 4:4-7 (New Living Translation)*

Thought:

When you are going through a situation that doesn't line up with the will of God expressed in Scripture, it's natural for anyone to want to make sense of it. We need to find purpose in the problem. We want to know a reason why. It's in our nature – our fallen nature – to want to make reasonable sense out of life. If we make sense of everything, where's our life of faith?

God has promised us a peace that passes understanding but how can we expect that if we worry about trying to understand everything about what we're going through?

from 10 minutes a day

God's peace passes understanding. Why would we want to settle for understanding?

Asking "Why?" usually gets our focus onto what God hasn't done. We point the finger at God and others. It's counter-intuitive for living un-offended at God.

So how do we get the peace that passes understanding?

1. Rejoice in the Lord always; again I will say, rejoice! (Philippians 4:4)

    The joy of the Lord is your strength. Choose joy despite the circumstance.

2. Let your gentleness be evident to all. (Philippians 4:5)

    Don't use your hurt as an excuse to hurt others. Too often we do that to those who are closest to us first and most. God is gentle with us, be gentle in your words and actions.

3. Do not be anxious about anything, but in everything, by prayer and petition, with thanksgiving, present your requests to God. (Philippians 4:7)

    Take all your concerns and leave them with God. Pray the Psalms if you need a good lament, but be sure to turn it back to the good things about God.

Wow, that sure seems like a good lesson to fast from negativity.

It does appear strange to give up the right to understand, but the secret is we can only make sense of some situations when we have the peace that passes understanding.

We don't get that peace by trying to understand.

True, at times we will make sense of some very negative events this side of heaven. It is the glory of God to conceal a matter, and to search out a matter is the glory of kings. (Proverbs 25:2)

But it's also true when we choose to live un-offended at God, sometimes understanding it all just won't matter once we have the peace that passes it.

Prayer:

Lord, I need the peace that passes understanding. I call on my Lord who spoke "Peace" to the storm and it obeyed. In my life there is a storm and I need You to change me or change my situation, or change both. Lord, I will rejoice in You always, my gentleness will be evident to all, and I will present all my requests to You with thanksgiving. You are good and You are great. Thank You, Lord.

Challenge:

Rejoice, be gentle, and take everything to God with thanksgiving. Live life with the peace of God that transcends all understanding.

Declaration:

I choose to live un-offended at God. I agree with the Bible that God is Good and God is Great. Even though I don't understand my circumstance, I give up my right to understand so that I can have the peace that passes understanding.

from 10 minutes a day

LIFE ABOVE the Negativity

Day 31 -
Do Not Allow
the Seed to Go to Waste

Truth:

> I tell you the truth, unless a kernel of wheat is planted in the soil and dies, it remains alone. But its death will produce many new kernels—a plentiful harvest of new lives. Those who love their life in this world will lose it. Those who care nothing for their life in this world will keep it for eternity. John 12:24-25 (New Living Translation)

Thought:

The seed needs to die before it has any potential. Many times we stand before God with a broken dream, unfulfilled vision or loss of a promise and it feels just like the plant we tended so carefully has just gone dry and withered.

It has.

But don't let the seed go to waste.

If you bury it and water it you'll get fruit. If you sit with it and stare at it and complain about it, you'll never get the divine justice that's due because of that loss. All you do is keep the wound open and ready for infection.

Divine justice repays a loss seven times (Genesis 4:15). That's what you're entitled to as a child of the king.

It doesn't do any good to hold a seed in your hand. Plant it, water it and look for divine justice.

What if I don't care about divine justice? What if I just hurt and don't want to choose to live un-offended at God? Does it really matter?

Look at what happened to Jesus at Nazareth in Mark 6:2-5

> The next Sabbath he began teaching in the synagogue, and many who heard him were amazed. They asked, "Where did he get all this wisdom and the power to perform such miracles?" Then they scoffed, "He's just a carpenter, the son of Mary and the brother of James, Joseph, Judas, and Simon. And his sisters live right here among us." They were deeply offended and refused to believe in him.

> Then Jesus told them, "A prophet is honored everywhere except in his own hometown and among his relatives and his own family." And because of their unbelief, he couldn't do any miracles among them except to place his hands on a few sick people and heal them.

Offense at God brings unbelief.

You may go through a season of pain, but don't let that season define your life. Don't let it rob you of your future. Plant the seed, turn the pain over to God, and trust Him to do what's right.

Water the seed – remind yourself of the truth of God's word. Insist on divine justice to repay you seven times for your loss. Know who you are in Christ and live out of the love God has for you.

Prayer:

Lord, release divine justice for every area the enemy has stolen, killed and destroyed. I put my trust in You to repay and to avenge. Lord, I want this seed to spring up and produce a harvest. I want victory in the areas I've seen defeat. I want You to be recognized as true to Your word. I know that is what You are. I know You give good gifts to Your children. I rest in Your peace knowing You'll make all things right.

Challenge:

Have you given way to unbelief in your life by choosing to take offense at God? Ask God to reveal any area where you have and agree with Him that what He reveals is sin. Ask for forgiveness and know you have been forgiven. Press in for divine retribution to be fully repaid.

Declaration:

I choose to live un-offended at God. I agree with the Bible that God is Good and God is Great. Even though I don't understand my circumstance, I give up my right to understand so that I can have the peace that passes understanding.

Day 32 -
Wield the Sword
To Stay Strong

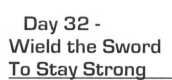

Truth:

> *I lift up my hands to your commands,*
> *which I love,*
> > *and I meditate on your decrees.*
> *Remember your word to your servant,*
> > *for you have given me hope.*
> *My comfort in my suffering is this:*
> > *Your promise preserves my life.*
> *Psalm 119:48-50 (NIV)*

Thought:

Jesus' words in John 16:33 were not meant to discourage us or say God is ever against those who obey Him. When He told us we'd have trouble in this world, it was a heads up to living in a fallen world.

Since we've all experienced trouble, and since we all know there is more seasons of trouble ahead of us, the question becomes "How can we go through trouble and abstain from negativity?"

The answer is to strengthen yourself in the Lord.

This is what David did when his men returned to Ziklag to find their wives and children captured and houses destroyed and the ones who would become David's "mighty men" spoke openly about stoning him. (1 Samuel 30:6).

from 10 minutes a day

LIFE ABOVE the Negativity

Over the next several days we'll look at various tools you can use to strengthen yourself in the Lord. Today we take a quick look at something most followers of Christ know they must use and very few know how to use effectively or appropriately – the living word of God.

There are three tools to remind you of, that relate to wielding the sword of the Spirit.

1. Let the Bible Read You

There are two big problems when it comes to our use of the Bible. First, we don't use it. It sits on the shelf and gathers dust. We are either intimidated to pick it up or bored with it because we think we've heard all the stories. In either case, it's an attitude of the heart we need to repent of. The Bible is our bread. It is the word that gives us life. We can't afford to not consume it regularly. Once you've repented, and in order to help you change your ways, make Bible reading a regular part of your day. We've included some Bible reading plans on 40DaysFromNegativity. com to help you.

But simply reading the Bible is not enough. We can gain knowledge of the Bible, but the Bible tells us "knowledge puffs up" (1 Corinthians 8:1). So how do you read the Bible so it has its intended effect on your life?

You let the Bible read you.

This is how you let the Bible read you.

    a. Approach with reverence

    b. Approach without intention

    b. Approach with expectation

Maybe I should explain... please forgive a longer

than usual daily encouragement... we're running out of 40 Days.

Approach with reverence –

I fell in love with history by reading the Bible as a child. I fell more in love with the Bible, the more I studied history. This is an ancient text we amazingly have at our disposal. And it's more than that – Jesus is called the word made flesh. There was nothing in his appearance that we should be drawn to him (Isaiah 53:2-5) and though He was very God, everyone knew Him as a man. The Bible reflects Christ in this way. Although 40 different human writers wrote it over 3000 years, it is the very Word of God. So don't allow your familiarity with the Bible to breed contempt for it. It is a living and active sword.

Approach without intention –

If you read the Bible to prove a point, you're missing the point. If you read the Bible to say you've read it, that's the only benefit you'll receive. If you read the Bible to find your next sermon, you'll miss the treasure God has hidden for you. When you read the Bible, it is a wonderful conversation between you and the Holy Spirit.

Approach with expectation –

Your only intention when you read the Bible should be to hear from God. Expect Him to speak to you from His word and He will. Ask yourself questions about the passage your reading: What did it mean for the first ones who read it? What does it mean for me? How can I apply it in my life? God will interact at your level of expectation.

from 10 minutes a day

When you let the Bible read you, you realize you don't consume it the Bible consumes you.

2. Meditate on the Word

Christian meditation is dramatically different from eastern meditation. The goal of eastern meditation is to empty oneself. The purpose of Christian meditation is to fill you up.

If you don't know what that means, but you do know how to worry, then you already know how to meditate on Scripture. When we worry we think over and over and over about fears. When we meditate we think over and over and over about faith.

Think about what the Scripture meant at the moment. Think about what it meant in the immediate context. Think about what it meant in the context of history. Think about what it meant in the context of church history. Think about what it meant for you in the past. Think about what it could mean for you in the future. Think about a picture you saw or can imagine that depicts its truth. Think about what it means for others. Think about how you could sing it. Think about how you could pray it. Commit the passage to memory. Meditation is like a cow chewing its cud. I hope you can see why.

3.Praying the Bible

In the course of these 40 days, we've gone over how to pray the Psalms. It's a great prayer book for us to pour out our laments to God and remember to praise Him in the middle of all kinds of trouble. To strengthen yourself in the Lord, I definitely recommend the Psalms.

But the Bible gives us vocabulary for every situation we face. Don't limit yourself to the Psalms. When you pray the Bible, you pray with authority because you know you're praying the will of God. When you pray according to His will, you know He hears you and you know you'll have what you've asked of Him.

My only warning here is to remind you to pray not only the words of the Bible, but the context of those words. And you'll only know the context as you spend the time reading the word.

When you need to strengthen yourself in the Lord, or if you need to keep your strength in the Lord, read, meditate and pray the Bible.

Prayer:

> *Lord, You've given me Your word so I can be thoroughly equipped for every good work. Thank You it is able to teach, rebuke, correct and train me. Holy Spirit empowers me to ensure that happens. I know that the Word of God renews my mind so that I'm able to test and approve what the good, pleasing and perfect will of God is. Forgive my lack of discipline. Help me to be consumed by Your word.*

Challenge:

It's not bad to have good habits but don't let habits create familiarity and familiarity breed contempt for the word of God. Read the Bible today and expect it to become alive to you.

from 10 minutes a day

Declaration:

I choose not to be discouraged. I choose to look to God instead of my circumstance. I choose to strengthen myself in the Lord.

Day 33 - Remembering to Remember

Truth:

> *"Whenever the rainbow appears in the clouds, I will see it and remember the everlasting covenant between God and all living creatures of every kind on the earth." Genesis 9:16 (New International Version)*

Thought:

In ancient times, a sign of a covenant was the one making the promise would turn the bow around so an arrow would face him, if it was "loaded." He'd pull the string and declare the oath. This was a way to say, "If I break this covenant, my life is forfeit."

God did exactly the same thing when He gave Noah and all creation the rainbow in the sky. It's as if He's holding the bow against himself every time the rainbow appears.

I love rainbows. They remind me to remember that God is really, really good.

When in this world we have trouble, or even when we choose busy-ness to rule in our lives, remembering to remember is the first thing we forget.

Let's never forget the power of testimony.

from 10 minutes a day

Marketing mavens know the value of a "social proof." You need to have testimonials of your products or services on your website. But for the follower of Christ, testimony is even more powerful.

Testimony literally means the "story, or report, of one." Testimony is powerful because it is immediate, direct and personal. It isn't a story about something or a report about what somebody else said or did. It's not a theory or hypothesis or hope. It is a personal description of your own direct experience.

So how often do you remember the good things God has done for you?

This is one area I need to improve on. God can bring to my memory incredible things He's done for me... and He often does when I wait on Him and listen to what He says. But most of the things I journal are in the dark days of my life. I write when I finally realize I can't do anything but cry out to God. And too often I forget to write down His answer. I know He answers because I know He's good and I know I'm facing new challenges today than the ones He helped me overcome... as some people say "new level, new devil."

Testimony is a powerful tool for us to use to remember. So keep a spiritual journal. What is God telling you today? What is He revealing to you? What verses came alive to you? If you keep track of your prayer requests, keep track of their answers as well. If you write out your laments like the Psalms, remember to praise Him for answers that have come. I often put updates in my personal journals but to do so; I need to remember to read the journal regularly. That may help you as well. Take time to remember by reading your journal.

Now testimony is great for us as individuals, but

its true power comes in community. If you have an accountability partner, hold each other accountable to talk about the good things God is doing. Be accountable for positivity. When there's opportunity to share in your church or on the street – make the most of it, remembering to do it with gentleness and respect. That's why you have a story to remember.

Your story influences others to trust God and praise God and turn to God in their own circumstance. It doesn't matter if you've been a follower of Christ for decades or have just begun the journey today, your story is important.

The most fun I have in life is to talk to new believers who bring newness to truths that I have taken for granted. Visiting with seniors who share their stories of God's goodness is also great… come to think of it – I like being around people who talk about the good things of God.

I need to be one of those people so people around me will be more like those kinds of people as well.

Will you be one?

Sharing with others your personal interactions with God enables you to strengthen yourself in the Lord.

Prayer:

Lord, help me to remember the good things You've done. Spirit, empower me to tell others about how good You are. I know it helps me to strengthen myself in You and I know it releases something in the heavens, because even angels long to look into the mysteries of God.

LIFE ABOVE the Negativity

Challenge:

Start a journal today, or write in your journal today. Make it a journal to remember the goodness of God. Record what you can remember from your past, or write down what God is revealing to you today. Write in it regularly and read it often... and if you ever imagine publishing for the glory of God, check out ImaginePublishing.com. I'd better use full disclosure here. ImaginePublishing.com is our publisher-for-hire company.

Declaration:

I choose not to be discouraged. I choose to look to God instead of my circumstance. I choose to strengthen myself in the Lord.

Day 34 -
Choosing Praise

Truth:

> After consulting the people, Jehoshaphat
> appointed men to sing to the LORD
> and to praise him for the splendor of his
> holiness as they went out at the head of
> the army, saying:
>> "Give thanks to the LORD,
>> for his love endures forever."
> 2 Chronicles 20:18 (NIV)

Thought:

When we face discouragement, many times the discouragement comes in the form of worry. So here are some quick steps to help you worry less and strengthen yourself in the Lord:

1. Isolate the worries that are on your mind the most. These are often the worries that we think about as we are falling asleep or as we wake in the morning.

2. Ask yourself specifically what you are afraid of. This will be the lie you are choosing to believe.

3. Ask yourself what the outcome would be of this specific fear coming true.

from 10 minutes a day

4. Ask God to show you the truth about the situation.

5. Ask God what He would have you do.

6. Expect God to answer you.

7. Replace the lie with the truth God revealed.

8. Obey what God tells you to do.

These eight-steps fit well with 2 Chronicles 20. Judah was facing three armies coming against them.

1. It was easy for them to isolate the worries. (v.2-4)

2. Jehoshaphat called out to God on behalf of the people and specifically voiced what they were concerned about. (v.10)

3. He looked at the outcome of the specific fear coming true (v.11).

4. He reminded everyone about the truth of God (v.6)

5. He ended his prayer with a cry we can all use: "We don't know what to do, but our eyes are upon you." (v.12).

6. A prophetic word came out as God's answer to the impending doom (v.15-17). This answer is also often ours – "You will not have to fight this battle. Take up your positions; stand firm and see the deliverance the LORD will give you." (v.17).

7. They worshipped God in response to His revelation, and then Jehoshaphat replaced the lies of the enemy with the truth of God by declaring, "Listen to me, Judah and people

of Jerusalem! Have faith in the LORD your God and you will be upheld; have faith in his prophets and you will be successful." (v.20)

8. Then they sent singers ahead of the army to praise God for who He is as they went out to obey what He told them to do (v.21).

The result for Judah was that there was no need to worry. God was in control. He set ambushes for the enemy and they destroyed themselves.

When we can get to the place of praising God for who He is before the things we worry about come to reality, they won't materialize.

Now I can hear the skeptic smirk, "most things people worry about never come about." True. So stop worrying completely by praising God continually. That's the 1-step program I intended to tell you about until God led me to 2 Chronicles 20.

Praise is our natural response to the goodness of God. When we see God as good, how can we worry about anything bad?

We can't. Strengthen yourself in the Lord by choosing praise.

Prayer:

Lord, I praise You now, even though I may not feel like it. Telling You the truth about Yourself reminds me how truly good You are. As I focus more on Your goodness my praise becomes more natural. You are good and Your love endures forever. You are good and Your mercies are renewed every morning.

LIFE ABOVE the Negativity

You are good and altogether trustworthy.
You are good. You are good. You are good.
You are good. You are good. You are good.
You are good. Thanks for being so good.

Challenge:

Read 2 Chronicles 20 and look for more of the treasures in this passage. Pray Psalm 86 and take extra time to praise God for who He is.

Declaration:

I choose not to be discouraged. I choose to look to God instead of my circumstance. I choose to strengthen myself in the Lord.

Day 35 - Standing in the Council of God

Truth:

But if they had stood in my council,
    they would have proclaimed my words
to my people
        and would have turned them from
their evil ways
        and from their evil deeds.
Jeremiah 23:22 (New International Version)

Thought:

There is one sermon I often hear preached that I just can't agree with. It is divisive to evangelistic outreach, ignores the context of Scripture and it's ignorant of the plans and purposes of God.

Yet the main point it makes is true… it's just based on the wrong text.

Now, don't lambaste your pastor if he ever preaches, "Don't have an Ishmael" because in this fast from negativity you should be in the habit of only speaking words that build up. It's not my intention to cause divisions with this illustration. Most preachers just don't read the text, God will hold them to account – you don't have to.

The basic premise of the sermon is, "don't get ahead of God." Great, I agree.

That's not what Abraham did though:

In Genesis 13 God told Abram his offspring would be like the dust of the earth – no one could count them. In Chapter 15 God confirmed the offspring would come from Abram's own body. In Chapter 16 Abram's wife Sarai offered her maidservant to fulfill a culturally legitimate function that God honored in the creation of the twelve patriarchs, two generations later. In Chapter 17 God finally told the newly named Abraham, Sarah would have a son AND that God would bless Ishmael (v.20).

That's really not the topic of today's thought, simply something we need to change in the church if we're ever going to see Islam go the way of Communism before Christ returns. God loves the children of Ishmael, and is waiting for their full number to come in.

"Don't get ahead of God" is a true message. Jesus only said what He heard the Father say and only did what He heard the Father do (John 5:19-20). Do you think Christ's times of getting away to pray had anything to do with it?

"Don't get ahead of God" isn't a license to stay stagnant. It's a challenge to listen and obey. When you stand in the council of God, He tells you the words to say, He gives you the love to show, He provides the strategies you need. (Jeremiah 23:22)

When we listen with expectancy, we hear the voice of God. When we hear God, we are encouraged. When we hear God, we are blessed. When we hear God, we know who we are. Waiting to hear the voice of God is another way to strengthen ourselves in the Lord.

So make the time to expectantly listen... then go until God says, "no."

Prayer:

Father, I come in the name of Jesus Christ with thanksgiving and praise. As I wait upon You now, I do my best to listen to Your voice. I stand before the almighty God and seek Your counsel. Please reveal any information that I need for today. Reveal any strategies that I need to employ right now. I need to be knowing and doing what You want.

Challenge:

Spend time in the presence of God. Expect Him to speak. Wait for Him to speak. Do what He says... it will always be in line with His will expressed in Scripture.

Declaration:

I choose not to be discouraged. I choose to look to God instead of my circumstance. I choose to strengthen myself in the Lord.

from 10 minutes a day

LIFE ABOVE the Negativity

Day 36 -
Pray in the Spirit

Truth:

> *But you, dear friends, build*
> *yourselves up in your most holy faith*
> *and pray in the Holy Spirit.*
> Jude 1:20 (New International Version)

Thought:

Did you ever notice Paul wished everyone would speak in tongues? Read 1 Corinthians 14:5 a little slower, and stop at the first comma. If you jump up to the verse 4 you'll see why... because the ones who speak in tongues build themselves up.

The context of 1 Corinthians 11 – 14 is that Paul is addressing problems that happen when the church is gathered. When you speak in tongues it's for God and yourself. It's not for other people (14:2) so it doesn't need to be done in a public gathering.

However, much of our public gathering today is focused on a personal intimate time with God. Since speaking in tongues builds yourself up, if it's appropriate in your church context, why not pray to God in an unknown language much like you would in a language that you've learned?

That's a side bar... let's get back to how to strengthen yourself in the Lord.

Paul taught the church in Rome:

In the same way, the Spirit helps us in our weakness. We do not know what we ought to pray for, but the Spirit himself intercedes for us with groans that words cannot express. And he who searches our hearts knows the mind of the Spirit, because the Spirit intercedes for the saints in accordance with God's will.
Romans 8:26-27 (NIV)

Allowing the Spirit to pray through us allows us to pray confidently knowing we intercede for others according to the will of God. It allows us to pray beyond words, because we don't know what to pray, but the Spirit Himself intercedes for us.

But is it for everyone?

In 1 Corinthians 12:31, 14:1 and 14:39, we are told to "eagerly desire greater" spiritual gifts. In the context of the passage, the greater gifts are the gifts that fit the moment. For example, prophecy is more desirable for a group setting, so seek to prophesy when you're together. Since speaking in tongues builds up the individual, we can assume when we're alone the greater gift is the gift of tongues.

Why would Paul want everyone to speak in tongues if it was not available to everyone? Why would he say to not forbid the speaking in tongues (1 Corinthians 14:39) if we all couldn't do it? Why are we told to build ourselves up as we pray in the Holy Spirit (Jude 1:20) if it's only available for some?

When you eagerly desire the gifts of the Spirit, it only takes a moment before you begin to operate in those gifts. The key is expectancy.

Luke 11:9-13 says:

So I say to you: Ask and it will be given to you; seek and you will find; knock and the door will be opened to you. For everyone who asks receives; he who seeks finds; and to him who knocks, the door will be opened.

"Which of you fathers, if your son asks for a fish, will give him a snake instead? Or if he asks for an egg, will give him a scorpion? If you then, though you are evil, know how to give good gifts to your children, how much more will your Father in heaven give the Holy Spirit to those who ask him!" (New International Version)

God is good and He gives good gifts to His children. Eagerly desire the gifts of the Spirit and the Spirit will give them.

So to strengthen yourself in the Lord pray in tongues if you've got them, seek them if you don't.

Prayer:

Lord, You are the giver of good gifts. I'm asking You for your best. I know in this life I need to build myself up in You and since the gift of tongues is the gift You've provided Your body to do just that, I ask You for this gift and I will eagerly pursue all gifts You give for the good of Your body and bride.

Challenge:

Most people's problem with speaking in tongues is psychological, not spiritual. We expect the Holy Spirit to possess us and move our lips. It rarely happens that way. God is a gentleman and won't impose His will on us. You're going to need to open your mouth. You're going to need to form words you don't understand with your lips. Since without faith it's impossible to please God, when you do this by faith, you know you're pleasing Him.

If you can already speak in tongues, pray using them for 20 minutes a day and see how strengthened you become over the next week.

Declaration:

I choose not to be discouraged. I choose to look to God instead of my circumstance. I choose to strengthen myself in the Lord.

from 10 minutes a day

Day 37 -
Change the Weather

Truth:

> *But the LORD said to Moses and Aaron,*
> *"Because you did not trust in me*
> *enough to honor me as holy in the sight*
> *of the Israelites, you will not bring this*
> *community into the land I give them."*
> *Numbers 20:12 (NIV)*

Thought:

God almost always punished the children of Israel when they grumbled against Him as they spent the 40 years wondering in the desert. There was one time He didn't. Instead He punished Moses – the one who interceded for the people time and time and time again.

It was the time Moses' reaction to the sin of the people was in direct disobedience to what God told him to do. Look at Numbers chapter 20. The people once again complained to Moses. He went before God and was told to lift up his rod over the rock. Instead he struck it twice and was told he wouldn't bring the people into the land of promise.

Seems a bit harsh, doesn't it?

Maybe we should see how seriously God takes our response to negative situations. Moses' reaction to the complaints of the people made him sin against God.

Do we ever allow our negative circumstances to let

us choose to sin against God?

One of the lessons God is teaching me through this negativity fast is I need to be careful how I react to actions, attitudes and spirits that set themselves up against the knowledge of Christ. When people who should know better seem to act under the spirit of stupor I want to confront them and challenge them and get them to see it right... I need to digress; I'm fasting from negativity and as you can see, I may have a way to go to make it a lifestyle.

I know how God wants me to react. I'll share more of that in about two days. But for now it's enough for you to know that how we react to those around us is important to God.

Moses couldn't enter the promise land because of how he reacted to the grumbling of the people of Israel.

So how are we to act positively in extremely negative situations?

The key is to practice the presence of God.

Brother Lawrence was a 16th century Carmelite monk and was the first to popularize this discipline. He saw God in everything. All his work was "as unto the Lord." He wrote in what would become "The Practice of the Presence of God":

> "As often as I could, I placed myself as a worshiper before Him, fixing my mind upon His holy presence, recalling it when I found it wandering from Him. This proved to be an exercise frequently painful, yet I persisted through all difficulties."

LIFE ABOVE the Negativity

Practicing the presence of God is focusing on His holy presence wherever we are, whatever we do. When you live within a negative environment, you need to live with the understanding given to us by JB Philips' translation of Romans 12:1-3:

"Don't let the world around you squeeze you into its own mold, but let God remold your minds from within, so that you may prove in practice that the plan of God for you is good, meets all his demands, and moves toward the goal of true maturity" (Romans 12:1-3; Phillips)

Don't use your negative environment as an excuse to remain negative. As a child of the one who created the weather, you bring your own weather wherever you go. As you allow God to renew your mind from within, you will begin to change the world around you.

You are the salt of the world and light of the earth. You preserve and illuminate the area where you are. The gates of hell cannot prevail against you so live the promise of Isaiah 26:3:

You will keep in perfect peace all who trust in you, all whose thoughts are fixed on you! (NLT)

Prayer:

Lord, I know it matters to You how I respond to other people's negativity. Forgive me for responding negatively

*myself. Help me, Holy Spirit, to recognize
the holiness of God wherever I go. Enable
me loving God to bring Your love, joy,
peace, patience, kindness, goodness,
faithfulness and self control wherever I go.*

Challenge:

Take up the 16th century challenge of Brother
Lawrence and as often as you can today, place
yourself before God as a worshiper and fix your
thoughts on His goodness and holiness. Bring Him
into your thoughts and conversation today.

Declaration:

I choose to change my negative environment by
seeking God and pursuing His peace.

Day 38 - Pursuing the Palpable Presence of God

Truth:

> You reveal the path of life to me;
>   in Your presence is abundant joy;
>   in Your right hand are eternal pleasures.
> Psalm 16:11 (HCSB)

Thought:

If you've been reading the articles I've written on how to fast from negativity, or listen to some of the podcasts available at LivingCreatively.revtrev.com, you'll know that I'm a big fan of spending time in the palpable presence of God.

Call it soaking, waiting, marinating, shut up and listen time, or whatever... I'm convinced it is a key for keeping in step with the Spirit and carrying only the burdens Christ has for us. It changes us so we can change our environment.

Pursuing the palpable presence is where you quit striving, you focus on the love of God and you expect God to speak. Let the word of God guide you. Let the music encourage you. Tell God you're waiting until you know He's released you to move on and you wait knowing He's going to speak and that you'll need to respond.

I don't know if Moses had the music, but he had the sentiment in Exodus 33:

from 10 minutes a day

> *Then Moses said to him [the Lord], "If
> your Presence does not go with us, do
> not send us up from here. How will
> anyone know that you are pleased with
> me and with your people unless you go
> with us? What else will distinguish me
> and your people from all the other people
> on the face of the earth?"*
> *Exodus 33:15-16 (NIV)*

It's not the power of God we seek; it's the presence of God that distinguishes us from all the other people on the face of the earth. In His presence there is fullness of joy and the joy of the Lord is our strength. It's in His presence that we can see things from His perspective. It's in His presence that burdens are lifted.

If we don't make time to experience the palpable presence of God we will not carry the yoke that is easy and the burden that is light.

Read how Eugene Peterson translates Matthew 11:28-30

> *"Are you tired? Worn out? Burned out on
> religion? Come to me. Get away with me
> and you'll recover your life. I'll show you
> how to take a real rest. Walk with me and
> work with me—watch how I do it. Learn
> the unforced rhythms of grace. I won't lay
> anything heavy or ill-fitting on you. Keep
> company with me and you'll learn to live
> freely and lightly." (The Message)*

That's the benefit of pursuing the palpable presence of God. Learn the unforced rhythms of grace. Learn to live freely and lightly. It is so great to make use of our rights as children of the King. Go spend some time on your Daddy's lap.

Prayer:

> *Lord, give me an expectant heart. I need to believe what Your word says is true – that I'll seek You and find You when I seek You with all of my heart. I know that as I wait expectantly on You, I'll renew my strength and rise up with wings as eagles. I'll run and not grow weary, I'll walk and not faint. Lord, teach me to wait expectantly.*

Challenge:

Make time today to cease striving. Be still and know that He is God. Play some worshipful music. Meditate on a passage of scripture. Focus on the love of God. Expect Him to speak.

Declaration:

I choose to change my negative environment by seeking God and pursuing His peace.

Day 39 -
Peace is the Proof
of Your Authority

Truth:

> Don't be intimidated in any way by your
> enemies. This will be a sign to them that
> they are going to be destroyed, but that
> you are going to be saved, even by God
> himself. Philippians 1:28 (NLT)

Thought:

When God places us as His salt and light in an environment that is extremely negative, our peace can change the weather around us. Peace isn't being self-assured; it's being assured that God is good.

Francis Frangipane wrote in an email concerning spiritual warfare:

> We will never know Christ's victory in its
> fullness until we stop reacting humanly to our
> circumstances. When you truly have authority
> over something, you can look at that thing
> without worry, fear or intimidation. Your
> peace is the proof of your victory.

The disciples were scared at the storm on the lake, while Jesus slept in peace (Matthew 8:23-27). When they woke Him up He didn't fight against the storm

from 10 minutes a day

or fear it. He used His authority in perfect peace.

When did Jesus ever argue with demons? Even satan was simply answered with truth.

Jesus was so calm as He stood before Pilate that in a matter of moments, it was no longer Jesus who was on trial, but satan, Pilate and the religious establishment in Israel.

Francis Frangipane continued:

> Satan's arsenal consists of such things as fear, worry, doubt and self-pity. Every one of these weapons robs us of peace and leaves us troubled inside. Do you want to discern where the enemy is coming against you? In the network of your relationships, wherever you do not have peace--you have war. Conversely, wherever you have peace-- you have victory. When satan hurls his darts against you, the more peace you have during adversity, the more truly you are walking in Christ's victory.

Paul told the Philippians:

> *Don't be intimidated in any way by your enemies. This will be a sign to them that they are going to be destroyed, but that you are going to be saved, even by God himself. Philippians 1:28 (New Living Translation)*

He's saying that our peace is a sign to others that God is in control and we're on the winning side.

You'll remember a couple of days ago I confessed I need to be careful how I react to actions, attitudes and spirits that set themselves up against the knowledge of Christ. I tend to get aggressive and confrontational. At least I did, until God decided to teach me more about peace. He's doing it by showing me Jesus.

Jesus was never in a hurry. He ignored ignorant arguments. He took time for people. He took time to laugh. Even the darkest moments He spent in prayer. He was overwhelmed with grief, but never crushed. He never used His circumstance as an excuse to step out of the will of God. It's tough to understand His peace.

That's the kind of peace I'm after and it's the kind of peace I get when I live out Philippians 4:4-8.

We'll conclude with Francis Frangipane's conclusion:

Rest precedes rule. Peace precedes power. Do not seek to rule over the devil until you are submitting to God's rule over you. The focal point of all victory comes from seeking God until you find Him, and having found Him, allowing His presence to fill your spirit with His peace. From full assurance at His right hand, as you rest in His victory, so will you rule in the midst of your enemies.

So seek peace and pursue it.

LIFE ABOVE the Negativity

Prayer:

Lord, I know You are the God of peace and have peace that passes understanding available to me as I rejoice, am gentle, am thankful and take everything to You in prayer. Spirit, help me to always fix my thoughts on what is true, and honorable, and right, and pure, and lovely and admirable. Help me to think about things that are excellent and worthy of praise so that Christ's authority in me can be seen.

Challenge:

Seek peace by seeking God. Allow His presence to fill you with His peace. Don't be intimated by people and circumstance. Spend time with God to be reminded He is good and He is great.

Declaration:

I choose to change my negative environment by seeking God and pursuing His peace.

Today's quotations were from:

Francis Frangipane Ministries of Francis Frangipane

Email: francis1@frangipane.org August 5, 2007

c/o ElijahList Publications 310 2nd Ave SE, Albany, OR 97321

www.elijahlist.com email: info@elijahlist.net Phone 1-541-926-3250

Day 40 -
<u>Do Everything In Love</u>

Truth:

> *We know what real love is because Jesus gave up his life for us. So we also ought to give up our lives for our brothers and sisters. If someone has enough money to live well and sees a brother or sister in need but shows no compassion—how can God's love be in that person?*
>
> *Dear children, let's not merely say that we love each other; let us show the truth by our actions. Our actions will show that we belong to the truth, so we will be confident when we stand before God. Even if we feel guilty, God is greater than our feelings, and he knows everything. Dear friends, if we don't feel guilty, we can come to God with bold confidence. And we will receive from him whatever we ask because we obey him and do the things that please him.*
>
> *And this is his commandment: We must believe in the name of his Son, Jesus Christ, and love one another, just as he commanded us.*
>
> *1 John 3:16-23 (NLT)*

Thought:

It's really difficult to say more about love than John does in his first letter. The man was passionate about love. I'm convinced it was because the church in Ephesus that he was an elder of was told by God

from 10 minutes a day

to return to their first love or else they would cease to exist.

I'm sure I wrote more about that somewhere and I'm sure it's really good stuff, but I can't find it in all this information that's been produced over these 40 days. In some ways, it has been a long journey so it's good to reflect on the final day and say with Qoheleth:

> That's the whole story. Here now is my
> final conclusion: Fear God and obey his
> commands, for this is everyone's duty.
> Ecclesiastes 12:13 (NLT)

What is God's command? – To love God and love others. Love is the fulfillment of the law. Love is the antidote to negativity.

We could have called this "40 Days of Love" and while it might have played better on Facebook, it didn't have that "come and die" motif that reflects the nature of the call of Christ.

"Love God, love others" sounds so simple, and it is. But if it were easy to love, why wouldn't more people do it?

The answer to that question is also simple. It means death to ourselves when we put other people's interests ahead of our own. It means death to ourselves when we change our negative thinking patterns. It means death to ourselves when we speak words of life and stop speaking words of death. It means death to ourselves when we reflect the goodness of God to the side of the world that's away from the Son.

And that's the kind of sacrifice Jesus is looking for.

He said in Luke 14:26-27:

> *"If anyone comes to me and does not
> hate his father and mother, his wife and
> children, his brothers and sisters—yes,
> even his own life—he cannot be my
> disciple. And anyone who does not carry
> his cross and follow me cannot be my
> disciple."*

Christ is worthy of a greater love than the earliest love, a greater love than the dearest love, and a greater love than the nearest love.

Will you give it to Him today and always?

Will you show your love for Him by the way you love others?

You've been doing it for 40 days. When you've messed up, you've confessed and God's forgiven you. You know how to do it and you know it can be done. You can do all things through Christ who gives you strength.

This is not the end of the journey. Stay on the path we've joined for this short time. If you need this encouragement for another 40 days, maybe daily emails will help. Go to 40DaysFromNegativity.com and sign up anytime to have these emails delivered to you daily.

So before we part, I want to pray for you. I know I've prayed it over you often in my times with God. It's Paul's prayer to the Ephesians:

> *I keep asking that the God of our Lord
> Jesus Christ, the glorious Father, may give
> you the Spirit of wisdom and revelation,
> so that you may know him better. I pray
> also that the eyes of your heart may be*

*enlightened in order that you may know
the hope to which he has called you, the
riches of his glorious inheritance in the
saints, and his incomparably great power
for us who believe.*
*Ephesians 1:17-19 (New International
Version)*

You are loved by God, so love loving others... He does.

Prayer:

*Lord, I thank You for all You taught me
and have shown me on this 40-day journey.
Specifically I want to thank You for (Fill
in the Blank). You are good and You are
great. I thank You. I thank You for Your
love. I thank You for Your mercy. I thank
You for Your grace. I thank You that You
empower me to love others in Your name.*

Challenge:

Celebrate God today. Take some time to go over Isaiah 58 and reflect on the fast you've just completed. Focus on the promises in that text. Know that great things are in store. Remember the things He's spoken to you or provided for you or shown you these past 40 days. Talk about them to others. Rejoice a great deal today.

Declaration:

I can do all things through Christ who strengthens me!

Appendix A -
Bible Reading Plans

The way you use this guide is to pick a column and read through it, day-by-day. What that means is you can read through the gospels by reading about 4 chapters a day, or the Psalms by reading slightly more. You can read through the New Testament in 40 days by reading about 15 minutes a day. That's the longest we've planned out for you here.

So pick a column and read it... you don't read every column every day.

Day	Gospels	Psalms	Major Prophets	Paul	NT
Day 1	Matthew 1:1-4:25	Psalm 1:1-6:10	Isaiah 1:1-5:30	Romans 1:1-2:29	Matthew 1:1-7:29
Day 2	Matthew 5:1-6:34	Psalm 7:1-10:18	Isaiah 6:1-10:34	Romans 3:1-4:25	Matthew 8:1-12:50
Day 3	Matthew 7:1-9:38	Psalm 11:1-17:15	Isaiah 11:1-16:14	Romans 5:1-6:23	Matthew 13:1-17:27
Day 4	Matthew 10:1-11:30	Psalm 18:1-19:14	Isaiah 17:1-22:25	Romans 7:1-8:39	Matthew 18:1-22:46
Day 5	Matthew 12:1-13:58	Psalm 20:1-23:6	Isaiah 23:1-27:13	Romans 9:1-10:21	Matthew 23:1-26:75
Day 6	Matthew 14:1-16:28	Psalm 24:1-27:14	Isaiah 28:1-31:9	Romans 11:1-12:21	Matthew 27:1-Mark 3:35
Day 7	Matthew 17:1-19:30	Psalm 28:1-31:24	Isaiah 32:1-36:22	Romans 13:1-14:23	Mark 4:1-8:38
Day 8	Matthew 20:1-21:46	Psalm 32:1-34:22	Isaiah 37:1-40:31	Romans 15:1-16:27	Mark 9:1-13:37

LIFE ABOVE the Negativity

Day	Gospels	Psalms	Major Prophets	Paul	NT
Day 9	Matthew 22:1-23:39	Psalm 35:1-37:40	Isaiah 41:1-44:28	1 Cor. 1:1-2:16	Mark 14:1-Luke 1:80
Day 10	Matthew 24:1-25:46	Psalm 38:1-41:13	Isaiah 45:1-49:26	1 Cor. 3:1-4:21	Luke 2:1-5:39
Day 11	Matthew 26:1-75	Psalm 42:1-45:17	Isaiah 50:1-56:12	1 Cor. 5:1-6:20	Luke 6:1-9:62
Day 12	Matthew 27:1-28:20	Psalm 46:1-49:20	Isaiah 57:1-62:12	1 Cor. 7:1-8:13	Luke 10:1-13:35
Day 13	Mark 1:1-3:35	Psalm 50:1-54:7	Isaiah 63:1-Jeremiah 1:19	1 Cor. 9:1-10:33	Luke 14:1-18:43
Day 14	Mark 4:1-5:43	Psalm 55:1-58:11	Jeremiah 2:1-4:31	1 Cor. 11:1-34	Luke 19:1-22:71
Day 15	Mark 6:1-7:37	Psalm 59:1-63:11	Jeremiah 5:1-7:34	1 Cor. 12:1-13:13	Luke 23:1-John 2:25
Day 16	Mark 8:1-9:50	Psalm 64:1-67:7	Jeremiah 8:1-11:23	1 Cor. 14:1-40	John 3:1-6:71
Day 17	Mark 10:1-11:33	Psalm 68:1-69:36	Jeremiah 12:1-16:21	1 Cor. 15:1-58	John 7:1-10:42
Day 18	Mark 12:1-13:37	Psalm 70:1-72:20	Jeremiah 17:1-21:14	1 Cor. 16:1-2 Cor. 1:24	John 11:1-15:27
Day 19	Mark 14:1-15:47	Psalm 73:1-75:10	Jeremiah 22:1-25:38	2 Cor. 2:1-4:18	John 16:1-21:25
Day 20	Mark 16:1-Luke 1:80	Psalm 76:1-77:20	Jeremiah 26:1-29:32	2 Cor. 5:1-7:16	Acts 1:1-6:15
Day 21	Luke 2:1-3:38	Psalm 78:1-72	Jeremiah 30:1-32:44	2 Cor. 8:1-10:18	Acts 7:1-10:48

Day	Gospels	Psalms	Major Prophets	Paul	NT
Day 22	Luke 4:1-5:39	Psalm 79:1-82:8	Jeremiah 33:1-36:32	2 Cor. 11:1-12:21	Acts 11:1-16:40
Day 23	Luke 6:1-7:50	Psalm 83:1-86:17	Jeremiah 37:1-41:18	2Cor. 13:1-Galatians 2:21	Acts 17:1-22:30
Day 24	Luke 8:1-9:62	Psalm 87:1-89:52	Jeremiah 42:1-47:7	Galatians 3:1-4:31	Acts 23:1-28:31
Day 25	Luke 10:1-11:54	Psalm 90:1-93:5	Jeremiah 48:1-49:39	Galatians 5:1-6:18	Romans 1:1-7:25
Day 26	Luke 12:1-13:35	Psalm 94:1-98:9	Jeremiah 50:1-51:64	Eph. 1:1-2:22	Romans 8:1-14:23
Day 27	Luke 14:1-16:31	Psalm 99:1-103:22	Jeremiah 52:1-Lam. 2:22	Eph. 3:1-4:32	Romans 15:1-1 Corinthians 6:20
Day 28	Luke 17:1-18:43	Psalm 104:1-105:45	Lam. 3:1-5:22	Eph. 5:1-6:24	1 Corinthians 7:1-13:13
Day 29	Luke 19:1-20:47	Psalm 106:1-48	Ezekiel 1:1-5:17	Phil. 1:1-2:30	1 Corinthians 14:1-2 Corinthians 4:18
Day 30	Luke 21:1-22:71	Psalm 107:1-108:13	Ezekiel 6:1-11:25	Phil. 3:1-4:23	2 Corinthians 5:1-Galatians 1:24
Day 31	Luke 23:1-24:53	Psalm 109:1-113:9	Ezekiel 12:1-15:8	Col. 1:1-2:23	Galatians 2:1-Ephesians 3:21
Day 32	John 1:1-3:36	Psalm 114:1-118:29	Ezekiel 16:1-18:32	Col. 3:1-1 Thess. 1:10	Ephesians 4:1-Philippians 4:23
Day 33	John 4:1-5:47	Psalm 119:1-63	Ezekiel 19:1-21:32	1 Thess. 2:1-4:18	Colossians 1:1-2 Thessalonians 1:12
Day 34	John 6:1-71	Psalm 119:64-176	Ezekiel 22:1-24:27	1 Thess. 5:1-2 Thess. 1:12	2 Thessalonians 2:1-2 Timothy 3:17
Day 35	John 7:1-8:59	Psalm 120:1-127:5	Ezekiel 25:1-28:26	2 Thess. 2:1-1 Timothy 1:20	2 Timothy 4:1-Hebrews 6:20

from 10 minutes a day

213

LIFE ABOVE the Negativity

Day	Gospels	Psalms	Major Prophets	Paul	NT
Day 36	John 9:1-10:42	Psalm 128:1-134:3	Ezekiel 29:1-32:32	1 Timothy 2:1-4:16	Hebrews 7:1-13:25
Day 37	John 11:1-12:50	Psalm 135:1-137:9	Ezekiel 33:1-36:38	1 Timothy 5:1-6:21	James 1:1-1 Peter 5:14
Day 38	John 13:1-15:27	Psalm 138:1-141:10	Ezekiel 37:1-40:49	2 Timothy 1:1-2:26	2 Peter 1:1-Jude 25
Day 39	John 16:1-18:40	Psalm 142:1-145:21	Ezekiel 41:1-44:31	2 Timothy 3:1-Titus 1:16	Revelation 1:1-11:19
Day 40	John 19:1-21:25	Psalm 146:1-150:6	Ezekiel 45:1-48:35	Titus 2:1-Philemon 25	Revelation 12:1-22:21

Appendix B -
Bible Memorization

"Your word have I hid in my heart, that I might not sin against you." Psalm 119:11. In our world of busyness we often don't take time to reflect. Memorizing Scripture is a wonderful way for us to meditate on it.

If you're new to memorization, rote learning is one way you can memorize. Say the verse over and over and it will eventually stick. If you're musical, put it to song. It's much easier to memorize and it gets into your inner person.

You'll know it's part of you when you pray it, and live it. Here are 10 verses you can memorize over the next 40 Days. With a little bit of effort, you'll own them in 4 days each. Enjoy. If you want to do more, memorize the verses we've started every day with.

Days 1 – 4

Again I say, don't get involved in foolish, ignorant arguments that only start fights. A servant of the Lord must not quarrel but must be kind to everyone, be able to teach, and be patient with difficult people.
        2 Timothy 2:23-24 (NLT)

Days 5 – 8

Your word is a lamp to my feet
    and a light for my path.
I have taken an oath and confirmed it,
    that I will follow your righteous laws.
Psalm 119:105-106 (NIV)

Days 9 – 12

Love is patient, love is kind. It does not envy, it does not boast, it is not proud. It is not rude, it is not self-seeking, it is not easily angered, it keeps no record of wrongs. Love does not delight in evil but rejoices with the truth. It always protects, always trusts, always hopes, always perseveres. Love never fails.
1 Corinthians 13:4-8 (NIV)

Days 13 – 16

You will keep in perfect peace
all who trust in you,
all whose thoughts are fixed on you!
Isaiah 26:3 (NLT)

Days 17 – 20

So think clearly and exercise self-control. Look forward to the gracious salvation that will come to you when Jesus Christ is revealed to the world. 1 Peter 1:13 (NLT)

Days 21 – 24

Can anything ever separate us from Christ's love? Does it mean he no longer loves us if we have trouble or calamity, or are persecuted, or hungry, or destitute, or in danger, or threatened with death? As the Scriptures say, "For your sake we are killed every day; we are being slaughtered like sheep." No, despite all these things, overwhelming victory is ours through Christ, who loved us. Romans 8:35-37 (NLT)

Days 25 – 28

Jesus said to the people who believed in him, "You are truly my disciples if you remain faithful to my teachings. And you will know the truth, and the truth will set you free." John 8:31-33 (NLT)

Days 29 – 32

Always be full of joy in the Lord. I say it again—rejoice! Let everyone see that you are considerate in all you do. Remember, the Lord is coming soon. Don't worry about anything; instead, pray about everything. Tell God what you need, and thank him for all he has done. Then you will experience God's peace, which exceeds anything we can understand. His peace will guard your hearts and minds as you live in Christ Jesus.
Philippians 4:4-7 (NLT)

Days 33 – 36
But if they had stood in my council,
    they would have proclaimed my words to my people
    and would have turned them from their evil ways
    and from their evil deeds.
Jeremiah 23:22 (NIV)

Days 37 – 40
You reveal the path of life to me;
    in Your presence is abundant joy;
    in Your right hand are eternal pleasures.
Psalm 16:11 (HCSB)

Booklet

The Freedom of Forgiveness

Unforgiveness is the greatest inhibitor of spiritual maturity in the body of Christ. Too many people don't understand what forgiveness is or the freedom that it brings. Learn what the Bible says about forgiveness and how to apply it to your life

How can I forgive others?

How do I ask for forgiveness?

How do I know that I am forgiven?

Do I need to forgive God?

This booklet is a primer to help you think the Father's thoughts about forgiveness and enable yc to work out its implications on your life.

1 for $3 | 2 for $5 | 10 for $

Booklet

Expect More Reading the Bible in a Year

This Bible reading plan allows you to read throug the whole Bible once and the New Testament twice in a given year. It was produced for a leap year, but since it only takes 15 - 20 minutes a day to read, you probably can squeeze in an extra day sometime even if you read it in a normal year.

It's great for staying motivate, and the monthly motivation is to meditate, not to race through the Word.

1 for $3 | 2 for $5 | 10 for $2

Howard C. Lund

Walking Through the Valley...

Written by Howard C. Lund in the last year of his time on this earth. His struggle will help you endure your struggles and give you great hope for the life that is to come that you can confidantly believe because it is promised by the Scriptures. It's a tribute to Howard's genuine faith and an encouragement to all who read.

Soft Cover 188 Pages
published through ImaginePublishing.com

$19.9

oward C. Lund

he Spotted and Wrinkled hurch

ritten by Howard Lund before his passing into
ernity, this book was completed by his son
evor. It is written to help the bride ready herself
r the coming of her bridegroom.

ft Cover   220 pages
iblished through ImaginePublishing.com

$17.99

) Days

ife Above the Negativity from 10 minutes a day

isting from negativity is a difficult thing to do. Let
is book help you keep every thought,word and
tion in agreement with the Father's.

ft Cover   220 pages
iblished through ImaginePublishing.com

olume Discounts Available
ecial Editions available for orders over 250.

$18.95

) Days

ilicon Bands

ese are motivators to stay positive. They are
rfect for snapping yourself when you have a
gative thought word or action. It's a great way
facilitate change and they are an open door to
are the postivity of Christ with those who ask
u what they are for.

'e have many more items like these - that help
u remember to stay positive and share your
cision at the same time. They are available in
ur shop at www.ExpectancyMinistries.com

1 for $1.50 | 10 for $13.50 | 100 for $98